Talking Turkey

And
Other
Stories
of North Carolina's
Oddly Named Places

Jamie Cox

DOWN HOME

Down Home Press, Asheboro, N.C.

ISBN 1-878086-82-0

Library of Congress Control Number
00-131808

Printed in the United States of America

Book design by Beth Hennington

Cover design by Tim Rickard

Down Home Press
P.O. Box 4126
Asheboro, N.C. 27204

for Caroline and Debo

Acknowledgments

I gratefully acknowledge that this book is made possible in part by a grant from the North Carolina Arts Council, a state agency, and the Arts & Science Council—Charlotte/ Mecklenburg, Inc.

I am indebted to the following persons for their encouragement, advice, and help in the preparation of this book: Belinda Hurmence, Carol G. Walters, Ethel T. Perry, Joseph Bathanti, and the Iredell County Writers' Group.

I am grateful to the many county historical and genealogical societies and groups who allowed use of information from their heritage books and materials. Their generosity and assistance have been invaluable. Specific credits to these groups and persons providing information are listed elsewhere in this book.

During research I became more aware of the many fine public libraries in this state. The staff of my home county library (Iredell, Steve Messick, director), with Margie Wessels and David Bunch, were very helpful. Kevin Cherry, librarian in the History Room of the Rowan County Public Library (Philip Barton, director), came to my aid on many occasions. Special thanks, also, to Mary Ruth Jennings of the Currituck County Public Library; Helen Causey, Moore County Public Library; Kim Viscounty, Franklin County Library; Ann Wright, Asheville-Buncombe Library; Marsha Haithcock, Randolph County Library; and Mitchell County Library staff who provided information gathered by Denise Stamey.

Thank you, Bill Harriett, for giving permission to use information from the *History and Genealogy of Jones County*, the publication edited and published by your late mother, Julia Pollock Harriett. Thank you, Gwyneth Duncan, volunteer researcher with the Orange-Durham Genealogical Society for your efforts. My thanks, also, to Ed Morris of the N. C. State Archives and to Dr. William S. Powell, author of the *North Carolina Gazetteer*, for replying at the start of this project with suggestions and encouragement.

Preface

Place names, especially North Carolina's, have long intrigued me. I must have been five when my mother and I visited the mountain community where she grew up. It was there, in the Cox's Chapel Community north of Sparta (actually over the line in Grayson County, Virginia) that I heard about the naming of Bridle, Saddle, and Horse Creeks.

The story went like this, as my mother recalled from her childhood:

A wealthy horse breeder in Grayson County owned a beautiful horse that he greatly prized. He planned to present this horse as a wedding gift to his bride-to-be, but before he could do so, the horse vanished. The owner realized a thief had taken the horse, and adding insult to injury, had stolen the horse's saddle and bridle, as well.

The irate owner gathered his friends and they saddled and rode off in hot pursuit.

They rode south into North Carolina, scouting each byway, path and stream, until they came to a fast-moving creek. They knew at that moment they were on the right trail, for hanging on a bush at the creek was the missing bridle.

They plunged ahead and came to a second creek some miles away and there—abandoned no doubt in haste so the horse could travel lighter and faster—was the missing saddle.

Encouraged, the pursuers galloped onward. They rode and rode and finally down in Ashe County, they came upon another clear mountain stream. On that creek bank stood the horse, bridle-less, saddle-less, and rider-less, contentedly munching on grasses at the water's edge.

Ever since that time, my mother said, those creeks have been known as Bridle, Saddle, and Horse. Well, what about the thief? I demanded. Where was he?

How disappointed I was that my mother didn't remember the thief's fate! For years afterward, I hoped to learn of "String-'em-Up" Creek, but never did.

A couple of years ago, I began a novel set in a small town I named Mercy, North Carolina. I went to the state map index of cities and towns to check on the existence of such a place. I did not find Mercy, which was fine, and even better, the name fit right in with actual place names of Trust, Faith, and Justice.

In the novel, I had the protagonist tell the origin of the town's name and as I wrote the fictional origin of Mercy, I realized that I wanted to know the honest-to-gosh origins of actual place names. Places such as Micro, Bear Grass, Old Trap, and Bandana. Places such as Welcome, Joe, and Toddy.

This book is the result of that idea. Originally, I planned to confine research to cities and towns listed on the state map index. How foolish of me!

How could I include Lizard Lick and leave off Dumpling Town simply because Dumpling Town didn't make the map listing? How could I write about Pilot Mountain and not of Standing Indian Mountain? How could I walk away from Black Ankle, Slapout, or Matrimony Creek?

I allowed research to grow beyond original plans and have included communities, creeks, and mountains—wherever I found an interesting story behind a name.

There are many intriguing names for which I could find no story, and many others that time would not permit the search. Wonderful names like Rudyatt, Greasy Creek, and Cutawhiskie Swamp. And Topknot, Tadmore and Vengeance

Creek. Quite likely, I will keep looking. I am hooked forever...

"The cat. He walked by himself, and all places were alike to him." So said Rudyard Kipling. Not true for human-kind, however. We love, respect, and honor places and our naming of them celebrates their differences.

Contents

Part I
What You Say May Be Used

Part III
Animal, Vegetable, and Mineral

Part 1

What You Say May Be Used

1
Out of Mouths

I have fallen in love with American names,
The sharp names that never get fat,
The snakeskin titles of mining claims,
The plumed war bonnet of Medicine Hat,
Tucson and Deadwood and Lost Mule Flat.
　　　　　—Stephen Vincent Benet

No-one can accuse North Carolinians of being shy or stingy about identifying our own with something other than generic terms. When we name a place, we just flat out up and call it like it is.

Take No Creek in southern Davie County. What happened was, an early settler bought some land in the area and expected right away to find the creek mentioned in his deed. He looked high and low and couldn't find the creek—remember that in those days not much underbrush clearing had been done.

The settler was mad as everything, which is a normal reaction for someone who feels that he hasn't gotten his money's worth.

"I've got no creek," he complained to everybody who would listen. He ran his mouth until his wife got aggravated and said, "Come on, honey, we're going for a walk and let you cool off."

They hadn't walked more than a quarter mile when the wife stopped in her tracks, pointed to a bushy lined stretch of land, and said, "Sounds to me like I hear running water over in them bushes."

The couple rushed over, parted the underbrush, and the settler said, "Well, whaddya know...."

Word got out, after the wife giggled and told a neighbor lady about catching some fish in "No Creek."

In Camden County, on the site of what once was an Indian village called Pasquenoc, is a community now known as Old Trap. In the eighteenth century this place's present name simply popped up one night, right from the lips of one of the local farmer's wives.

A popular tavern stood near a windmill and bay where farmers brought their grains and met trading vessels on the Pasquotank River. Many farmers would transact business and stop by the tavern for a few drinks before going home.

Wives were not happy with this custom.

On one particular night, a farmer visited the tavern after his trading and arrived home late—very, very, late.

"Sorry, sugarbabe, but I had mule trouble," he said.

"Mule trouble, my foot," she squawked. "Smells to me like you've been lolly-gagging down at that cotton-picking old trap."

Well, she may not have said cotton-picking, but this is the historical fiction version of how Old Trap got its name.

Ever hear of Redbug? Ever wonder why it's called that? Ever visit there long enough to figure it out?

It is said that this community in Columbus County (another community in Brunswick County bears the same name but spells it with two words) got the Redbug name this way:

A long while back a fellow built a tavern in a settlement that was still unnamed. This rural area in Eastern North

Carolina has a mild climate and apparently all the attributes which encourage zillions of teensy biting redbugs to make their homes there.

When the tavern owner went into Whiteville to get his business license, he had just walked around the wooded area of his property. He no more than sat down with the licensing clerk when he felt the sting of a redbug bite.

Scratch, scratch.

"And what is the name of your location, sir?" the clerk asked. "We can't issue a license without a place name."

Scratch, scratch.

"Doggonit," the tavern owner exclaimed, "just put me down as being from Redbug."

Today if you travel Sampson County on NC 242 about one mile north of Salemburg on State Road 1414, you'll come to a spot where a general store used to be.

The store and storekeeper are long gone but the area nickname—Slapout—remains.

It's told that the storekeeper was a master of inefficiency—at least, in the inventory department. Oh, he kept basic stuff like matches and brooms and kerosene, but mostly his shelves were lonesome-looking.

He always acted surprised, though, if a customer came in and inquired for something that he didn't have. He acted as if the item should be right there on the shelf, but by some rare misfortune it wasn't. "Why, you sure caught me at the wrong time," the storekeeper would say. "Right now I happen to be slap out."

It got to where folks just grinned and said, "Well, before we make a trip to town, might as well waste a little time and stop at old Slapout."

Also in Sampson County (the northern part at the western edge of Newton Grove) is the community with the nickname of Easy Street. The place is at the highest elevation in the county—at the headwaters for Great Coharie, Mill Creek and Seven Mile Swamp.

According to storekeeper Alfonzo Godwin, Easy Street got its name from a chance comment.

During the Great Depression, Godwin owned a general store across the road from a store he later ran with his wife, Lola. The store was a popular place for folks to socialize, buy things, and stay cool, especially during sweltering eastern Carolina summers.

The store's concrete floor, in those days before air conditioning, was the coolest place around. One day a group of field-hands came in for a bottle of pop and a short break from the heat. The whole crew took their pop bottles and stretched out on the floor.

Uncle Frank Maynard stopped by the store about the time everybody was stretched out swigging on their big orange drinks, grapes, Dr. Peppers and Coca-Colas. He wasn't exactly everybody's uncle but he had lived in the area a long time and folks called him that. One thing about Uncle Frank, he'd say whatever came to mind.

He looked at all this relaxing and took a deep breath.

"Looky here, now," he said, "I sure must have stumbled on Easy Street."

Once upon a time in what is now Surry County, there lived an Indian hunter who was extremely skillful with a bow and arrow. Problem was, he knew it and couldn't keep his mouth shut for bragging.

Naturally, other hunters got sick and tired of hearing this fellow say how good he was—how he could bring back meat to the camp anytime he chose, how he could use an arrow to kill any large animal and have that animal drop mortally wounded on a designated spot, blah, blah, blah....

The other hunters decided to call the braggart's claim,

and not long after that, a hunting party spied an elk which had wandered down from the mountain and was drinking at a nearby stream. They knew the elk had superb senses of sight, smell, and sound so they figured the animal would be long gone before they got within arrow range. Seemed like a good time to put an impossible challenge to the boasting brave.

"Put your arrow where that big talk is," they taunted. "Drop that elk in the water, if you're as good as you say you are."

The expert hunter took steady aim, released the arrow with powerful ease, and the elk dropped into the stream.

"Elk in," said the marksman calmly, buffing his fingernails on his deerskin vest.

From then on the stream was known as Elkin Creek and later on the town of Elkin took the name of the creek.

Of course, this tale about the name may not have been what really happened. We don't know a single soul who was there that day.

2
A Word Here and There

George Washington wasn't in the business of naming places, but that's what happened at Comfort, according to Jones County tradition.

During President Washington's southern tour, he stopped in Trenton on April 22, 1791, and had dinner at a tavern known as the Shingle House, or Weber House, according to some records. After dinner, Washington continued his trip, stopping for the night sixteen miles down the road at Shines Inn.

Now, George had been having something like a Goldilocks journey, in that his sleeping accommodations thus far hadn't been up to snuff (you did know he used, didn't you?). Anyway, first one bed would be too soft, then another too hard, and it wasn't getting any better. But George was being pretty stoical about it—the way he'd been concerning creature comfort since Valley Forge.

So when he signed in for the night at Shines Inn, he expected no more than a fitful night's sleep. He stretched out on the bed (likely plumped with a feather tick), did a little stretching and found that the bed wasn't too soft, nor was it too hard. Matter of fact, it was just right. George slept like a log.

The next morning innkeeper Shine asked his guest how he slept. "In comfort, my friend," George Washington said, giving a contented sigh, "in comfort."

• • •

The father of our country was by no means the only person to turn a descriptive word or phrase that settled in and became a place name.

A spectator attempting to break up a fist fight led to Gap Civil, which was an earlier name for the Alleghany County town of Sparta.

Before Alleghany County formation, The Gap was a village outpost in Ashe County. The mountain gap is located between Sparta and Twin Oaks and the first post office there (1825) was called Bower's Store.

Some years later, in the 1840's, a quarrel began one afternoon and ended with a brawl in the village street. All that rowdiness got to a fellow standing by. "Cut that out," he yelled, "This is a civil place."

That comment made such a hit that in 1846 residents changed the post office name to Gap Civil. It remained Gap Civil until June 24th, 1879, when the name was changed to Sparta. Who chose Sparta, the name of the ancient Greek city-state, isn't documented. But like Alleghany County Sparta, old Sparta was located on a plateau surrounded by mountains. And some say this name was chosen because ancient Sparta's citizens were known for their hardy self-discipline.

Sam D. Campbell was a busy man during his lifetime. He was a building contractor and real estate dealer who helped build the old Piedmont Wagon Company's factory in Hickory.

Campbell owned a nice home and some land west of Hickory in Catawba County and frequently walked around his property and over to the Southern Railway tracks nearby. Which is what he was doing, with friends, one afternoon in the early 1900s. Campbell and his friends stood and gazed down the long, straight railway tracks covering the miles to Hickory. "It's a long view, fellows," Campbell said to his friends.

Later, in 1907, when the town there was incorporated,

it was named Long View.

Before the Revolution, the McDowell family from Virginia settled in what is now known as McDowell County. "Hunting John" McDowell owned a particularly fine farm of spectacular beauty and fertile bottom-land soil. One day while he was out hunting on his property, he paused on a hill overlooking the rich fields below. He turned to his hunting companions. "These are indeed pleasant gardens," he said.

Pleasant Gardens became the name of McDowell's farm, and later the name of a McDowell County town. (The county was named for Hunting John's son, Joseph McDowell, who was a Revolutionary War hero at the battle of King's Mountain.)

In Onslow County, one community had early names of Oak Grove and King's Chapel. But when it was incorporated in 1880, it became Richlands, a name many had called the place for years because of the fertile land around the headwaters of the New River.

Try saying "Wootonton" several times in a hurry. No wonder that name proposed for a Columbus County town never flew. The name was to honor John Wooton, who once owned the town lands.

The name that did last is Fair Bluff. Men who rafted lumber down the Lumber River would tie up at a high bank on the south side of the river. This high rise where the town developed, the rafters said, was a "fair bluff."

The Shakerag district of Person County has been called that since the 1800's. All because of a militia captain of the district, William (Stoker Bill) Daniel, who named it after his men's shabby clothing.

Stoker Bill was a relaxed sort of leader, it's told, whose first word of command for the day was, "Fall up in a lump."

His second command was to his lieutenant, directing roll call. Roll call cleared the way for Stoker Bill's third and final command for the day, which was for his men to join him at the liquor stand.

Small wonder that one Hiram Satterfield in a March 8, 1887, newspaper account of Captain Daniel and how Shakerag got its name mentioned this: "We have heard some of the old men say they had rather muster under Capt. Daniel than anybody else—all they had to do was to attend the roll call and then repair to the liquor stand."

Early residents of Winfall in Perquimans County were a word-efficient sort. Consider how they selected their place name in 1775. A huge windstorm had recently blown in and caused the corner store to fall down.

Which is not to say that the namers of the first post office in a certain Davie County town were any less word-efficient. "We'll call it Advance," they said, "because having a post office located here will advance our community."

The same goes for Handy in Davidson County. The residents of this community were evermore happy when they got their very own post office! Before, they'd had to go three miles west to Jackson Hill to pick up their mail. Now, mail delivery was "handy."

Haoe Mountain is in western Graham County near the Tennessee line. Haoe, in case you're not familiar with the name, is pronounced "hey-yo." Folks started calling the mountain that after they learned pioneer settler John Stratton climbed the mountain one day, looked down into Tennessee, cupped his hands and called out, "Hey-yo."

Not getting any reply, he turned around, looked down into North Carolina, and repeated his call. If anybody answered this time, Stratton didn't tell about it.

3
Scary or What?

Not that the name Woodstock is all that scary sounding—unless you were a parent during a certain generation. But Woodstock is said to be a ghost town beneath the waters of the Pungo River, near Winsteadville in Beaufort County. Woodstock was the county seat of Hyde County until 1790. The courthouse burned in 1789 and the county seat moved the next year.

Folks tell of seeing the remains of the old courthouse at low tide off Woodstock Point. And if your eyes were open to such things, perhaps seeing in those shimmering waters some reminder of a supposed-to-be witch they said was burned at the stake in old Woodstock. She was accused of putting a spell on a small boy who died.

Hearing about Burnt Rock Ridge in Graham County could be a little spooky, if you're the nervous type. Way back in 1871, some hunters traveling along the ridge stopped and built a big campfire to warm themselves in the chilly mountain air.

They were safety-conscious, of course, and built the fire on some rocks so it wouldn't get out of control. But it did. The hunters, who had dozed off, awoke to the sights and sounds of a roaring blaze burning a great hole in the rocks.

Naturally they skedaddled, scarcely taking time to gather their possessions. The fire burned for days and so ferociously that thick smoke hung in the air for miles around. Chickens squawked, got confused and went scurrying home to roost. And to top it all off, no-one was ever able to explain why the fire burned so vigorously and so long.

If you plan to visit Graveyard Ridge in Haywood County, you might rather go in broad daylight. Not that any human remains have ever been found buried there. But with that name, diggers have looked into grave-resembling mounds found in a flat area along the ridge.

The theory is that many hundreds of years ago a tremendous windstorm uprooted a lot of trees on the ridge. Time rotted the old stumps leaving dirt mounds. The slight depression beside each mound may be the hole where the stumps were.

While we're talking graveyards and the like, let's speak of Fools Bridge Township in Greene County. Got its name from Fools Bridge across an actual stream there. Which got its name like this:

When the bridge was built, one end happened to rest in a cemetery. Which meant, of course, that bridge users had to go through the cemetery to get to other destinations. This didn't set well with one jumpy fellow who avoided the bridge entirely at night. It didn't matter if taking the long way around did make him late to things, he said. No way was he traipsing through that cemetery at night. In fact, he said, only a fool would.

The name of a Dare County spot didn't scare off the Wright brothers in 1903. They made their first successful flight from Kill Devil Hills. Most agree that the name had something to do with a popular rum consumed by locals—a brand of

Medford Rum, so strong some said it would "kill the devil." William Byrd, of Virginia, in 1728 wrote in *History of the Dividing Line*, "Most of the rum they get in this country comes from New England, and it is so bad and unwholesome, that it is not improperly call'd Kill Devil."

The devil himself is supposed to visit Devil's Tramping Ground in Chatham County. Maybe not every night, but when he does he walks in a circle and schemes to overcome the good of the world and work his wicked ways. Proof of the devil's circular walks, say those who think they have it figured out, is that nothing will grow in the devil's walking path. How long has it been here? Forever, they say. It's enough to raise a goose pimple.

The Devils Garden on the Blue Ridge Parkway (on the Alexander and Wilkes County line) grows a good crop of copperheads and especially healthy rattlesnakes on its rocky terrain. Wouldn't you just expect that from the devil?

A natural rock formation looks like the devil. Literally. You'll find Devils Head near Chimney Rock in Rutherford County. The Devils Den is a small cave on Pilot Mountain in Surry County. A steady breeze blows from the cave. Hot air? From *way down* below?

On the lower Cashie River in Bertie County winds a bend so sharp it once was known as Devil's Bend. Before the Revolution, sailing vessels had to lower their sails and be pushed around the bend with pikes. Later, steamboats had such problems with the bend that they had to cut their engines to navigate the turn.

In Transylvania County, the Devils Courthouse is a black rock mountain rising steep and sharp-peaked. Devil's Race Path Branch in Avery County got its name because a long time ago some evil doings, maybe even a murder, took place there.

• • •

And another place in Avery County, well, this fellow named Whaley, back in the early days, went out roaming one night—must have been up on Dark Ridge and probably close to End of Nowhere Branch—because he got more spooked the further he went. In fact, he got so scared that when a screech owl let out that high-pitched racket of his, Whaley hid in a hollow log until a search party rescued him. Folks laughed a little about what Whaley did, but they liked him, and ended up calling a whole community Whaley.

If you're the jittery type and roaming around North Carolina, something like this could happen to you:

You take this notion to prove how brave you are and you talk two buddies into going with you to spend the night on top of Scream Ridge in Macon County. Now, your friends are not excited about this idea, but they agree, and off you go, all whistling and talking about what a great time you're going to have in the peace and quiet. It's still daylight and it's not like you're traveling along Spooks Branch over in Buncombe County.

You walk on and twilight fades to black. The terrain gets steeper and a little fog drifts past and brushes dampness across your forehead. Not much talking now, except somebody mentions it's getting chilly.

About that time, it happens. The sound. Rising from who knows where, or who knows what source. Low at first, moving to ear-piercing intensity and then gone, quickly as begun.

"Sounded like a ha'nt to me," says one buddy in a voice that cracks.

"Ain't no such things as ha'nts," you say, though the hairs on the back of your neck are frozen straight-up stiff.

Your other buddy's flashlight beam is doing a bobbing Maco Light, except it's the wrong county. But he speaks up.

"Sounded to me like one of those wildcats," he says.

"Probably ain't no wildcats left in this country," you say. You never did know when to keep your mouth shut.

The scream, or whatever else you want to call it, comes again. And with it, the scuffle shuffle of moving feet and a chilling realization.

Which is, your buddies have taken off and left you standing all by your lonesome on top of Scream Ridge. While they've headed out to their mamas' loving arms or the state line, whichever comes first.

4
Good Enough Reason

Montezuma. Brings to mind Aztec treasures and the exotic, doesn't it? More exotic, anyway, than Bull Scrape, which was the original name of this Avery County community.

Bull Scrape was a literally perfect name for that early place and time. Because of many unfenced lands, cattle roamed freely and frequented a salt lick set up at a mountain gap. Bulls huffed and puffed and got into scrapes before deciding who licked salt, and the gap is still known as Bullscrape Gap.

The community of Bull Scrape became Aaron when the post office came in 1883. Aaron was probably the name of the first postmaster. But in 1891, the place incorporated under a new name—Montezuma.

The naming of Montezuma was apparently an exercise in reverse, forward, or gear-crunching psychology. At least that's how it worked out.

The committee appointed to select a new name for Aaron decided on West End. They thought they understood human nature. If we offer only one name, they told each other, there'll be some in the crowd who'll complain and say they don't like it and what about something else? Let's give them another name as well, one we know they wouldn't have on a Christmas tree, like, uh, like, let's say, "Montezuma."

No contest. The citizens chose Montezuma.

• • •

If you consider the number of place names that happened because somebody visited a general store back in the early days, you could get the idea that a lot of people came up with names by visiting general stores.

Consider Falcon. It is officially listed in Cumberland County, but when the town was chartered on March 6th, 1913, a large portion of its corporate area extended east of South River into Sampson County.

Actually, Falcon had its beginnings in 1878 when William Culbreth and his partner, Captain James L. Autry, both of Sampson County, bought 259 acres which lay around Starling Bridge over South River. Culbreth established a store at the west end of Starling Bridge and soon folks were affectionately calling Culbreth "Cheap Bill." Not because of a character flaw, though. Culbreth priced his merchandise reasonably and people appreciated that.

It was one of William and Nancy Jane Culbreth's sons, Julius A. Culbreth, who in 1893 suggested Falcon for the name of the new post office at Starling Bridge.

Julius was a banker in Dunn at the time. He was visiting his father's store and a group of men were sitting around talking about what to name the post office. Julius picked up a box of Falcon safety pins. "Falcon is a nice name," he said.

We have forgotten the name of the railroad conductor, who, in 1890, renamed Chaplin's Stand in Davie County. But we haven't forgotten the name he gave it. Bixby. Here's how it happened:

One day when the train stopped at Chaplin's Stand, the conductor hopped off and went in the general store. Somebody said howdy and what did he think the new name for the station and place ought to be?

The conductor looked around and saw a large supply of Bixby Shoe Polish on one of the shelves. "I like that polish," he said. "Why not call the place Bixby?"

• • •

Wilkes County's Daylo didn't get its name from a visitor to a general store. It came from the store's owner. In 1924, E. N. Vannoy named the place for a brand of flashlights he sold.

One more time. A community in eastern Vance County and northern Franklin County was once called Dukes Crossroads, then shortened to Duke. When the post office was established in 1881, Simon W. Duke was to be the first postmaster and wanted to continue with the Duke name, but another post office (in Nash County) already had that name. So, what to choose?

Dr. Bennett P. Alston had the solution. He was sitting in the general store with some folks talking about the name change. He looked around and spied boxes of Epsom salts on the shelves.

"Bet we've all used some Epsom salts at one time or the other," he supposedly said. "Let's call the place Epsom."

Another doctor came to the rescue when a community in Montgomery County needed a name for its new post office and everybody was in a tizzy over what it should be. "What about a name nobody else is going to think of?" Dr. F. E. Asbury asked. "What about Ether?"

When Hinklesville got its first railway station, the residents of this Davidson County community also decided they needed a new name to go with the new station. A big welcome sign hung out front of the general store. One resident put the community's feelings into words: "Everybody's welcome here, so let's call the place Welcome."

Some places have taken the name choice of least resistance. The story about Aho is that when this community in

Watauga County needed an official name, a group of men got together to decide it. They sat and sat, talked and talked, but nothing creative happened. Finally somebody suggested that the next word spoken would become the new community name. The others nodded in agreement and silence reigned. They sat and sat, and one or two may have catnapped, until finally one man got up and stretched.

"A—ho," said B. B. Dougherty. And everybody smiled.

It was before the Civil War that a post office was assigned to the southern part of Randolph County. Local citizens needed to decide on a name. The good news was that a lot of people were interested in being in on the selection. Bad news was that there were as many name choices as people and nobody wanted to compromise.

One weary soul finally stood up during a chorus of "Why not this?" and "Why not that?" and said, "I'm ready to go home. Let's call the place Whynot."

Wondertown is a community near the town of Erwin in Harnett County. When this community developed, residents decided they wanted an identity of their own. Somebody suggested Erwin II, but that didn't seem to typify a new identity. "It'll be a wonder," somebody said, "if we ever will agree on a name."

A fellow of few words labeled No Business Mountain in Cleveland County. That was back in the old days, before many folks knew much about the almost unexplored mountain.

Joe, the fellow of few words, was asked by his buddy, Charlie, if he wanted to climb the mountain.

"Nope," said Joe.

"You chicken over eyeballing it with a bear?" Charlie asked.

"Nope," said Joe.

"You 'fraid we'll get lost and freeze to death?" asked Charlie.

"Nope," said Joe.

"Well, blast it," Charlie fussed, "why won't you go?"

"Got no business up there," Joe said.

5
More Good Reasons

Is there a North Carolinian who hasn't heard of Lizard Lick? Or one version of how Lizard Lick got its name?

Situated in Wake County between Zebulon and Wendell, Lizard Lick community developed in the 1800s. It later became known as Lizard Lake, then Talton's Crossroad, but the community reclaimed its original name in the 1960s.

Some of us who are lizard-cautious know a little about lizards, and for us, a little is enough. We've heard that lizards have good hearing and sight. And we'll accept on good authority that lizards can see colors. We've seen the lizard's long tongue, but we assume he uses it more for flicking insects out of the air than for licking, although it may appear otherwise to a casual observer. One thing we know for sure is that we don't intend to get close enough for him to lick us with it.

All versions of the origin of the Lizard Lick name say that way back lizards regularly sunned themselves on a rail fence near a local still. This became a convenient way to give directions to those looking for whiskey.

"Go down there to that fence where the lizards lick and you'll find a drink close by."

Another version is that a fellow with a walking stick visited the still and liberally sampled his purchase before making his way back home along the path beside the rail fence. He was feeling so good that he was twirling his walking stick. Occasionally, he would interrupt his twirling to take a lick at the lizards on the fence.

There wasn't much entertainment in Lizard Lick at the time, so this performance was not only noted but preserved in the community's name.

A Wayne County community was once called Sauls Crossroads for the Sauls family who owned large tracts of land there. But Sauls Crossroads wouldn't do when the post office came. The name was too long for the postmark.

Since many post offices were being established in those early days, finding a name that wasn't too short, too long, or already in use could be a problem. It was becoming one at Sauls Crossroads, until a local schoolteacher came up with a solution.

"Eureka," the teacher announced enthusiastically, "that's the perfect name for the new post office. That's Greek meaning, 'I found it,' which is just what I've done."

Aurora, in Beaufort County, was once called Betty Town but was renamed by its founder, the Reverend W. H. Cunningham. He wanted the place called Aurora because he said the town would be a "new light in the east."

Of course, others say that Aurora, incorporated in 1880, was renamed for a former county newspaper, the *Aurora Borealis*.

The naming of Hamlet in 1873 was a tree-jumping event, by accounts. This community was in the Sandhills of Richmond County. John Shortridge, formerly of England and transplant to the Sandhills was talking with three friends, Laughlin McKinnon, Thomas Steele, and Elisha Terry.

Shortridge enthusiastically spoke about the numbers of people moving into the settlement and told his friends that before long the place would be large enough to be called a hamlet.

In England, Shortridge went on to explain, a hamlet was a growing cluster of families and houses well on the way to becoming a full-fledged village.

We agree, said his friends, and furthermore, we think we should start calling this place Hamlet. To celebrate this occasion, the men planted a small sycamore tree in an area later known as Bridge's Triangle and jumped over it for luck.

The tree stood in Hamlet until 1946 when it was cut down to make room for construction.

In Franklin County, the community called Alert was settled about 1900. Thomas D. Farrow was the first postmaster and responsible for the name. "Folks around here are honest, God-fearing and alert, and Alert ought to be the new name," Farrow wrote on the name-application form that the postal department approved.

Unofficially, the original name of a Granville County town may have been Need More. But was this the proper image for a growing and prosperous town? Residents didn't think so. The place was incorporated in 1895 as Creedmore, then reincorporated in 1905, as Creedmoor. (This spelling *had* appeared in an 1887 atlas.)

The store that Henry Venters and his father owned and operated in Pitt County sold more colorful calico cloth than any other store around. Its reputation as the county calico capital suggested the name given to the post office and the community: Calico.

They call it Traphill, this community in northern Wilkes County east of Little Sandy Creek. The name came about when the post office was established in 1837. Everybody knew then about local resident William Blackburn, who regularly set a railpen snare for wild turkeys on a nearby hill.

• • •

Record keeping had to do with the naming of Yancey County's Daybook and with Ledger in Mitchell County.

In the early 1800s, a Mr. Chandler had a trading post in Yancey County. He sent mail by wagon train to immigrants moving west and the wagon trains brought mail back home from those who'd moved away. Mrs. Chandler kept records of mail in a large daybook, and folks eagerly checked the book for messages. Around 1815, the place took on the official name of Daybook.

A Mr. Phillips, in Mitchell County, applied to the powers-that-be in Washington for a post office in an isolated part of Mitchell County. Not enough mail coming and going to justify a post office, authorities told him.

That was enough to get Phillips riled and determined to prove his point. He kept a ledger of all the mail coming in and going out of the community for nearly a year. When he was satisfied with his proof, he mailed the ledger to Washington. The authorities were impressed, approved the post office and named it Ledger.

What were they listening for on Listen Knob? Why, this was where foxhunters built fires on this Caldwell County mountain peak and listened for their dogs running foxes.

Back in 1775, Joseph Pittman, who lived near a creek in Carteret County, did not take kindly to finding a thief making himself at home in Pittman's sweet potato patch. Pittman hollered and waved his gun at the thief, who ran, swam across the creek and jumped out on the other side. Safely on the creekbank, or so he must have thought, the thief turned to Pittman and shouted insults.

"Turn again and say what you did," Pittman shouted at the thief, who did just that. Pittman shot him.

They say that's how Turnagain Creek got its name.

6
It Happened Here

When the railroad came to the Toe River in the western part of mountainous Mitchell County, it was time to select a name and exact location for a new station.

Choosing the site fell to some of the railway workers who would be traveling the route, so they got together, went up and down the route, and found just the right spot. Too bad no-one had thought to bring anything to mark the chosen place.

No use cutting down brush to indicate the site, it would just grow back or somebody would mistake the downed brush for a place trampled by a bear. And with so many trees, there was no use trying to describe certain ones.

"Need something like a flag, something colorful, so it can be seen," said a member of the party. "And something that won't matter if it gets wet. I can't believe we came off without a thing to at least hang on a bush."

"What about this?" asked a railway brakeman. He reached up and untied the red and white bandana from his neck. "Be glad to let you have this—just tie one end to that laurel bush over there and sorta spread it out so that bright color can be seen. It's pure-tee cotton cloth, so won't matter if it gets wet."

Turned out the bandana was the perfect marker for the site. In fact, before it was all over, the group decided to use Bandana for the name of the new station and the community that would grow around it.

···

About 1748, a group of hunters from Pennsylvania came to a spot in Alamance County and camped in the dead of winter. Snow was on the ground, but the hunters cut trees for shelter and firewood. The next year, several of the hunters brought their families to live at the site, and remembering that first winter visit named their new settlement Snow Camp.

In February 1781, Cornwallis and his army also camped here during a heavy snow. Snow Camp is about midway between the Research Triangle and the Greensboro-High Point-Winston-Salem Triad.

A couple of communities in McDowell County owe their names to construction work. While building a road on what is now 226 South, workers had to blast their way through a hill of solid stone. Ever since, that area has been known as Rocky Pass.

As for the other community, builders of the Clinchfield Railroad laid a section of track over a bog. The main engine laying the track mired up and had a struggle getting freed. From then on, folks called the place Mud Cut.

Kilmarlic is a community whose boundaries rarely are described the same way twice. It is in Currituck County, somewhere along the eastern boundary of the Currituck Peninsula bordering Currituck Sound—perhaps as far north as the dividing line between Jarvisburg and Powells Point, and to the south as far as Halls Harbor and Payne's Swamp.

How Kilmarlic got its name is as indefinite as its boundaries. It could be that long ago, a ship carrying whiskey from Kilmarlic, Scotland, sank and the cargo washed ashore. All aboard the ship were lost, so what were local residents to do with all that perfectly good liquor? A good time was had by all and the event remembered with the Kilmarlic name.

That version is nonsense, some say. Maybe a ship did

sink, maybe a whiskey cargo did wash ashore, maybe a few folks consumed it. But they didn't enjoy it.

These were people who had regular access to West Indies rum, brought to the area by ship captains such as Elijah Evans, Willis Freeman, and many from the Hayman family. And we're being told residents got excited over musty tasting scotch whiskey? Enough to name the place for the event? Hmph...

According to the Jarvis family whose roots are deep in Kilmarlic earth, family tradition has that Honorable Thomas Jarvis, Esq. and his family sailed south from Virginia around 1652 to Port Roanoke (Roanoke Inlet). They came up the sounds to a hamlet called Kilmaic on Powells Point where they settled.

If the Jarvis tradition is correct, then Kilmaic is probably an Indian name, and Kilmarlic a corruption of it.

On Balsam Mountain on the Haywood-Swain County line is a place called Black Camp Gap. Long ago someone built a loghouse camp there for the use of cattle rangers and hunters. Then a forest fire swept through charring the logs of the cabins. For a long time after the fire, anybody who stayed in the cabins got soot and char markings on them. The place got the permanent name of Black Camp.

An Indian village was the first settlement at the foot of the Sauratown Mountains near the Dan River. It is now the present site of Danbury, county seat of Stokes County. During the 1790s an Indian trading post flourished there and the place became a bustling frontier town. Some say this early town was called Crawford. Others say the Crawford name didn't come until 1851, when the town was named that in honor of the wife of John Hill. Hill was a long-time clerk of court and member of Congress.

In 1852, one story says, commissioners were appointed

to select a more centrally located seat for the county—to re-place Germanton. The commissioners went on a selection expedition and chose a flat ridge near Cascade Falls. On their way home, they stopped in Crawford and had a few drinks at the Old Moody Tavern.

Well, maybe more than a few. By the time they left, they were so enthusiastic about the whiskey and the tavern, they decided to move the courthouse to Crawford and change the name of the town to Danbury for the nearby Dan River.

But another story says Danbury replaced Germantown as county seat in 1849 when the county divided to form Forsyth County. And that in 1852 the town became Danbury after the name of Governor Alexander Martin's plantation home. Martin was governor at the time Stokes County was created.

Captain Roger Haynes built a fancy home in New Hanover in the southeastern part of the state before the Revolutionary War. The home was so fancy, in fact, that folks called it Haynes' castle. Eventually, the area around became known as Castle Haynes, but you know how people are. They get lazy when they speak and drop letters. So the town is now known as Castle Hayne.

In Clay County, Couch Gap got its name during Civil War times. Draft dodgers, they say, hid (couched) under the cliffs and existed on the plentiful wild hogs. Clay County's Chairmaker Branch got its name because a man (whose name has been forgotten but not what he did for a living) made chairs there.

Robert Henry, surveyor (and doctor, some say) as well as Revolutionary War veteran, made a name for Clay County's Compass Creek. Henry was out surveying when he dropped his compass. Unfortunately, he dropped it while crossing the creek and watched in disgust as the instrument moved swiftly and forever away.

7
Looks Like

A turkey tail. That's what residents of a Burke County settlement thought an old tree root in their settlement resembled. So they started calling the place that. Later, when they decided that name had to go, they switched to Sigmonsburg in honor of a local storeowner. But they weren't really happy with that name either. Not until somebody came up with the name Glen Alpine, meaning beautiful valley, were they finally satisfied.

The town of Star in Montgomery County is said to be the geographical center of North Carolina. Who says? Well, the *Montgomery Herald* newspaper, for one.

The place started out being called Hunsucker's Store, a name that gave first postmaster Angus Leach writer's cramp. When postal authorities gave Leach permission to change the name, he picked the shortest name he could think of: Star.

Another version of the story has Leach in a storekeeper's role and says he suggested the name because the town's elevation made the place easily seen from all directions.

In 1775, early settlers in northwestern Caldwell County got together and cleared a large circular area from the wilderness to make way for homes and the settlement they hoped to establish. Most likely it was a schoolteacher in the bunch saying something like this that suggested the place name:

"Why, this big round clearing we've made here looks like a globe." Globe it became.

On top of a bald peak in Clay County in the far western part of the state is a large, unusual rock with a hollow in the top. Scrapings show that the hollowing happened long ago. The Cherokee have an explanation. The rock was the big pot used by a Cherokee medicine man to steep the medicinal herbs he used for healing. Today we call the peak Potrock Bald.

Potrock is not the only rock to have made a name for itself. We have Blowing Rock in Watauga County, which in spite of what the name suggests, doesn't do any huffing and puffing. This rock formation juts over a gorge through which John's River flows, and a frequent breeze supposedly returns to sender any light article, such as a handkerchief, thrown from the rock.

Chimney Rock, in Rutherford County, rises more than two hundred feet above the mountainside on which it perches and overlooks Hickory Nut Gorge and Lake Lure. There simply was no reason to call it anything other than what the granite monolith looked like—a chimney. The town of Chimney Rock flourishes nearby.

Centuries ago the Cherokee Indians used a smooth granite site in Henderson County for a ceremonial ground, which accounts for the town's name of Flat Rock. Flat Rock Playhouse, the state theater of North Carolina, now occupies the site.

Another Flat Rock community in Surry County may be called that because of a large granite quarry which was in operation as early as 1889. There is also a Flat Rock community in Stokes County and a Flat Rock Mountain in Avery County.

Charles Connor and George Masa were early residents of Swain County and could look out their windows anytime and see the Smoky Mountains. One day they were standing at the fence dividing their property and talking about nothing in particular when George looked over in the direction of a bumpy-looking mountain peak.

"Looky over there, Charlie, at that old mountain. What does that crookedy shape remind you of?" he asked.

Charlie studied the peak a bit and rubbed his chin. "I'd say it looks like a bunion on Old Smoky's foot," he replied and grinned.

George told a lot of people about "Charlie's bunion." It wasn't long before the mountain was being called Charlie's Bunion Mountain. It is on the line between Swain County and Sevier County, Tennessee.

Nearly everybody who has ever looked at the outline of Grandfather Mountain agrees that it is properly named. No-one remembers who first saw the profile of an old man (some suggest it looks like Abraham Lincoln, beard and all) and called it Grandfather. The mountain is at the junction of Avery, Caldwell, and Watauga counties.

And Grandmother Mountain is in Avery County, but why it is called that is unknown.

Erosion, rather than volcanic action, accounts for the shape of a unique peak in Surry County, perhaps our most distinctive mountain. The Saura Indians called it Jomeokee, meaning Pilot or Great Guide, and used it as a landmark as well as a symbolic guide pointing to the Great Spirit and Happy Hunting Ground.

The first white settlers continued to view the mountain, which rises more than 1500 feet above the countryside, as a landmark but called it Mount Ararat, or Stonehead Mountain. Today we know it as Pilot Mountain.

The town of Horseshoe in Henderson County sits on a

sharp bend of the French Broad River. The town of East Bend in Yadkin County was named for a nearby east bend of the Yadkin River.

In the old days, the road to a settlement in Alexander County from Iredell County was along Third Creek. No bridge offered easy crossing, so travelers found the shallowest spot and used it as a regular ford. This ford became known as the "stoney point on Third Creek." A village grew there but later in the nineteenth century, when a new road was established from Statesville to Taylorsville, the village moved to be near the road.

That wasn't the last move, though, for the village of Stony Point. Around 1885, when the railroad came, the village moved to a location a couple of miles east, taking it away from the original spot on the creek.

Stumpy Point community in Dare County is opposite the Pea Island Wildlife Refuge. Most likely colonists from the Outer Banks settled on this rounded point of land on the west bank of Pamlico Sound. Nobody really recalls why it was called Stumpy Point, but someone probably suggested that it looked like one.

In 1858, Jesse Brown became owner of land in Guilford County through which, in 1863, the Richmond and Danville Railroad built a line. The station was named for Brown. And because his farm was the highest point on the line, the name became Browns Summit.

Climax, also in Guilford County, is situated on high ground, which accounts for its name.

8
In Other Words

"No me da una discuenta?"

"Il n'est sauce que d'appetit."

So what connection does Spanish for "Won't you give me a discount?" or French for "Hunger is the best sauce" have with North Carolina place names?

Very little, but one uses what one knows.

Now that's cleared, let's consider some of our place names coming from other languages. Swannanoa, for instance, which is only one name of hundreds from our Native American heritage.

Swannanoa actually began as Cooper, named for A. D. Cooper who provided the land for this Buncombe County town. Settlers decided later to call it after the Swannanoa River which runs through it. That Swannanoa is an Indian word is agreed upon, but not its exact meaning. Did it once mean "beautiful" in the Cherokee language? Did the Indians intend the sound of the word to be like raven wings rapidly flying, as some suggest?

Or is it a name corruption of "Shawano" from the Shawano tribe, who had a small settlement at the mouth of the Swannanoa River? Or a word corruption of Cherokee "Suwali-Nunna," meaning "trail of the Suwali tribe?"

Whatever the meaning, frontiersman David Crockett liked the Swannanoa area. He courted and married a widow,

Elizabeth Patton, here. And he and Mrs. Crockett continued to visit her Buncombe County relatives for the rest of their lives.

Hertford County's Ahoskie may come from the Tuscaroran Indian word "Ahotskey," or "Ahoskie," meaning "Dead Horse Creek." It could be fact that Tuscarorans used a nearby creek for water in skinning horses for meat and hides.

Chocowinity is the name of a Beaufort County town, and one translation from Tuscaroran is "fish from many waters." Or perhaps the original word for the town was Chockowinekee, meaning "smoking stumps."

Tuxedo is the closest pronunciation we've managed from the contraction of Indian words "p'tauk-suttough" meaning "the place of the bears." Tuxedo is in Henderson County near another favorite bear haunt, the community of Bear Wallow.

And Saluda, in Polk County, got its name from the Indian word "salutah," meaning "Corn River."

"Vale of the Lilies" is our translation of the Indian word "Kullaughee," which became the name of Jackson County's Cullowhee. In early May, the lilies bloom in Cullowhee. Pure white blooms, with yellow stamens of brightest yellow, making a showy stand in their foot-high clumps.

About Cerro Gordo, in Columbus County...was E. P. Holmes right some years ago when he said the place was named by two train travelers from Cerro Gordo, Mexico? Holmes suggests the men got off the train, admired the location, compared it similarly to their homeplace, and suggested the name. In Spanish, Cerro Gordo means "large round hill."
Could be, though, that the date of the Battle of Cerro

Gordo during the War with Mexico coincided with the date the railway track being built west reached this location.

There is a Scottish word, sometimes spelled "foody" and meaning "a little crazy," which may be the origin of Mecklenburg County's Fuda Creek. The creek starts in Mecklenburg, wanders about a bit, and flows into Cabarrus County. Then again, the French word *fou*, pronounced "foo" means "crazy," also.

Ah, Sans Souci community is in Bertie County. The name comes from a plantation once located there. It is French and means "carefree, without worry."

We'll never know, perhaps, whether Lockwoods Folly Inlet got its name from Mr. Lockwood's foolishness or not. The inlet lies between Holden Beach and Long Beach in Brunswick County, with Lockwoods Folly River flowing through it into Long Bay of the Atlantic Ocean.

They say that in the seventeenth century, Mr. Lockwood built a large boat up the river. Measuring and marking turned out not to be Mr. Lockwood's strong suit. He huffed and puffed and pushed and wiggled his finished boat, but the dad-gummed thing was too large to float through the inlet to the Atlantic. Well, he was too disgusted and tuckered out by that time to cut it down to size, so he left it to rack and ruin. Naturally, he didn't refer to the project as a "folly," but others did.

That might not have been the true story, though. After all, the seventeenth century was a while back. The French word "folie" (delight or favorite place) may have accounted for the Folly part.

Back then, you see, it was common in England for people to use "Folly" (their version of "folie") in naming estates. Picture this possible scenario: Mr. Lockwood was from

England. He built his dream home on the banks of a beautiful river and lived happily ever after at Lockwood's Folly.

No-one remembers who put the French twist on Durham County's Red Mountain when the town became known by that name. They combined the French "rouge" (red) and "mont" (mountain) to make the name of Rougemont.

Valdese is a town in Burke County settled in the late 1800s by families from Italy. In Italian, Valdese means "Valley of our Lord."

Suppose you had the desire to visit Liberia, or Bolivia, or Arabia, but couldn't take time for extended travel? How about visiting places with other country names right here in North Carolina? You can, you know.

In fact, you can go to Little Switzerland—if you try McDowell County—and see mountain scenery reminiscent of that country. New Holland is in Hyde County.

North Carolina's Liberia is in Warren County. Bolivia is the county seat of Brunswick County (county seat used to be Southport but was moved to Bolivia sometime in the 1970s), and Arabia is in Hoke County. Scotland Neck, a town settled by (surprise, surprise) the Scottish, is in Halifax County.

As for finding the names of foreign cities in the names of North Carolina places, are you ever more in luck.

Oxford, England? Try Oxford, N. C., the county seat of Granville County, named in a roundabout way for Oxford, England. Early settler Samuel Benton named his plantation "Oxford" for the English place and the N. C. town was built on land from that plantation.

Manchester, England? Visit Manchester, near Spring Lake in Cumberland County. Sidney? Just don't be picky and insist on spelling the name Sydney as the Australians do. You'll find Sidney in Beaufort and Columbus Counties.

Actually, a passel of foreign city names exist in North Carolina, with many being named for places from which settlers came. Here is an additional sampling:

Lisbon (Portugal) is in Bladen County, Dublin (Ireland) in Bladen County, Aberdeen (Scotland) in Moore County, Belfast (Ireland) in Wayne County, Belgrade (Yugoslavia) in Onslow County, and Janeiro (Rio de Janeiro, Brazil) is in Pamlico County.

You've missed Berlin (Germany), though. That place name fell from favor during World War II. But the same pleasant place exists today in Ashe County with a different name, Bina.

The town of Morven is in Anson County, named for Morven, Scotland, home of the mother of Hugh McKenzie, who was the first postmaster.

Tunis (Tunisia) is located in Hertford County, Naples (Italy) is in Henderson County and Wagram in Scotland County. The other Wagram is in Austria.

Which reminds us that Austrians are not the only people who can waltz around Vienna. North Carolina's very own Vienna is in Forsyth County.

Part II

Love, Honor,
and Other Good Stuff

9
Thwarted Love

Poor Chunky Gal. When it was over, all that remained for her were memories and a namesake mountain.

Chunky Gal was an Indian girl who lived long ago near Shooting Creek in Clay County. Being a little plump—but delightfully so—she caught the eye of an Indian brave and the couple fell in love.

The bad news was that the brave was from a tribe in Macon County, and his tribe and Chunky Gal's got along about as well as the Hatfields and McCoys.

"No way," said Chunky Gal's father when she confessed that she wanted to marry her Macon County love. I don't care how big his campfire is or how many arrows are in his quiver. No daughter of mine is getting hooked up with that bunch from Macon County."

Well, Chunky Gal had a mind of her own. She sneaked out of camp and met the brave. "I'm sick and tired of my daddy telling me what I can do," she told her sweetheart. "Now, you gather some extra venison jerky, roll up a bunch of nice rabbit skins, and come over late tonight. When I hear you give a hooty-hoot call three times, I'll come out and we'll run away."

That's exactly what they did. They ran and ran until it was daylight and they had reached the big spring at a mountain gap. They sat down there to rest.

BIG MISTAKE. It was there Chunky Gal's father and a posse of braves overtook them.

Father insisted he knew best, and a tearful Chunky Gal went home without her Macon County true love. Forever after, the brave told all who knew him how he left his heart in Clay County on Chunky Gal Mountain.

A similar but sadder tale is that of the beautiful Indian princess Estatoe and a young warrior from the Watauga region.

The warrior was traveling through what is now Mitchell County when he chanced upon Estatoe picking berries in a meadow. They spent some happy hours together and fell hopelessly in love.

Knowing that their families would oppose the romance, the lovers eloped.

But someone had spied on the couple and soon Estatoe's father and brothers were in furious pursuit. They captured the pair at a cliff overlooking a mighty river.

Estatoe screamed in anguish as her brothers snatched the warrior from his horse and thrust a heavy spear through the young man's heart. She turned in desperate grief and threw herself from the cliff into the swirling waters below.

Some say the Toe River where Estatoe drowned was once called "Estatoe River" by her guilt-stricken family. (Horton Cooper, in his *History of Avery County North Carolina* begs to differ with the Indian princess version of the Toe River name. Cooper says the name came from the South Toe River that was named for a Mr. Towe, who visited and traded with the Indians and hunted in the lower Toe River Valley.)

There is a Mitchell County community on Brushy Creek, though, which is named "Estatoe," allegedly for that girl of long ago.

Paint Rock in Madison County is a sheer 100-foot cliff overlooking the French Broad River. Red stains on the rock's surface inspired the name.

For the scientifically inclined, the explanation for the red stains is iron oxidation. For romantics, there is this:

Again, Indian lovers from different tribes were forbidden to marry. Rather than live without each other, the couple jumped to their deaths from this cliff. The rock became forever stained with their blood.

A tidbit about Paint Rock, which has absolutely nothing to do with lovers, is that the place got some notoriety in 1855. Two Asheville men, John D. Hyman and Dr. W. L. Hilliard, fought a bloodless duel here. Hyman was editor of the newspaper *Spectator* and had printed criticism of the mail service. Dr. Hilliard, who was postmaster, got plenty ticked off and challenged Hyman to a duel. Hyman accepted and the men chose Paint Rock as the dueling site.

Fortunately, the duel ended after one round of rifle fire, with the only damage done being to a clipped-off button from Hilliard's coat.

Lovers Leap—a high point above the Hiwassee River in Cherokee County—and Lovers Leap Ridge—between Silvermine and Pump Branches in Madison County—have names that suggest similar ends to stories of frustrated lovers.

Around 1802, thwarted love drove David Grier to a bald-topped peak in Yancey County. The peak is forty-five miles from Asheville and visible from Roan Mountain. You'll hear the peak called Big Bald today, but some folks know that it was once called Grier's Bald.

David Grier came to the mountains in the late 1700's from South Carolina and made his home with Colonel David Vance, who had a beautiful daughter. David Grier fell in love with Miss Vance, but she did not reciprocate.

His love's lack of enthusiasm didn't stop David Grier. He persistently courted Miss Vance for four years, until...until...she up and married someone else.

David Grier was distraught. He grabbed a few belongings and took off into the wilderness. He plunged into unexplored territory with the same determination with which he had courted Miss Vance, not stopping until he had reached the bald summit of the mountain peak. Standing on the summit he decided to make a permanent home in one of the mountain coves. So, twenty miles from civilization, David Grier cleared a nine-acre tract and built a log house.

Isolation must have been enjoyable to Grier for he lived in his log home many years. But eventually settlers began to move into the wilds and Grier became upset about others coming to the area he felt was his alone. He quarreled over land rights with a settler named Holland Higgins—and killed him.

At the trial, Grier pled insanity and the court cleared him. He returned to the mountain but died at the hands of one of Higgins' friends.

If you're the sort who seeks out messages from unhappy love stories, you could find at least two among the stories just told.

One is that if you and your lover are fleeing a posse, avoid all cliffs.

The other? Doing yourself in is a really hard way to acquire a place namesake.

10
Honoring Her

In Rutherford County the brass bell inscribed "Given to the town of Ellenboro in loving memory of Ellen Robinson by her father—1874" is gone.

For many years it hung at the Ellenboro School and went along each time the school changed location. But in the early 1940's the bell disappeared, and some residents today believe that it was sold during those World War II years as scrap metal for military use.

The Robinson family was from Hamlet and Mr. Robinson was an engineer for the railroad that came to this area of Rutherford County in 1874. The place was fast becoming a shipping center for a mineral called Monazite and a community soon developed. The depot and community needed an official name. Would it be Monazite?

Mr. Robinson heard of the name search and approached the citizens. His daughter Ellen was terminally ill, he told them, and he wanted to do something that would be a permanent expression of his love for her. If they would consider naming the village Ellenboro, he would give them a brass bell. They agreed and Robinson kept the bargain.

There are those who confirm the existence of a bell but believe that Ellenboro was named by a local property owner, Burwell Blanton Byers. They say that Byers named the place for himself and his wife, Ellen. His name selection, "Ellenburwell," later became Ellenboro.

Another father, this one in Currituck County, honored a daughter in 1907 when he named a new post office Bertha. The place was originally known as Gall Bush Ridge because of many gall bushes growing there, but this name was too cumbersome for the new postmaster, Appolas Owens. After all, the post office was housed in his store and the postal department told him to assign a name.

Owens had several daughters, and we don't know why he chose Bertha. Perhaps the other daughters were not yet born. Another daughter, Pattie Robertson, became postmaster of Bertha in 1926, after Appolas Owens retired and moved to Florida. That post office closed in 1956, following the death of Pattie Robertson.

A Mitchell County community was originally called Magnetic City because of its iron ore deposits. But the first postmaster had the option of changing that name to something more to his liking. He chose his daughter's name and dubbed the new place, Buladean. The problem, if there is one, is that we don't know the postmaster's last name. Was his daughter named Beulah Dean? Or as others suggest, was the daughter's name Beulah and she married a Dean?

First postmaster Higgins, whose first name is unknown, named the Alleghany County town of Ennice in honor of his daughter in 1883.

And a Mr. Setzer, who was the first postmaster of a Haywood County valley community, named it Maggie in 1909 in honor of his daughter, Maggie Mae Setzer. We now call it Maggie Valley.

• • •

Texas McClelland was the daughter of Isaac and Lucy McClelland and her papa had a lot to do with her being named Texas. But do you think he called her that? No way. He called her Texana. Finally, just about everybody else called her Texana, too. Texana grew up and married Henry McAdams and they were the first to move into a settlement high on a mountain about a mile north of Murphy in Cherokee County. Texana became the name for this community.

A man who honors his mother-in-law may be a rarity. But this is exactly what Simpson B. Tanner, Sr. did in 1887 when he founded the community of Henrietta with the establishment of Henrietta Mills in Rutherford County. Henrietta McRae Spencer was his mother-in-law.

Tanner attempted to name another Rutherford County community that he helped establish directly north of Henrietta for his wife, Caroline. But the post office department said that Caroline was too similar to Carolina and would cause confusion. Tanner agreeably changed the name to Caroleen.

Stanley Martin, first postmaster of Spring Creek in Pamlico County, changed the community's name to Florence in honor of his wife.

The founders of Onslow County's Verona chose the name in honor of Vera McIntyre, wife of one of the builders of the Wilmington and Onslow Railroad. The first post office here was built in 1862 and called Aman's Store. The name changed after the railroad came along.

The first post office in Currituck County was named in 1904 for local citizen, Mamie Crank.

Miss Blanche Moore, niece of D. G. Watkins, was

honored by having a Caswell County community named for her because her uncle owned the land where it developed around 1875. Somehow the "e" got dropped from the community's name.

Another community in Caswell County is named Purley in honor of early community resident, Miss Purley Cobb.

Were Lizzie and Lillie one and the same female? The town of Lizzie in Greene County was originally called Lizzie's Store after a store that was built there in the late 1800s. Tradition says that shortly before the turn of the century, the place was also known as Lillie. Were Lizzie and Lillie sisters? Twins? Unrelated business partners? Nicknames for a lady named Elizabeth? Or none of the above? The answer remains a mystery.

In Clay County, you'll find Julie Knob atop Julie Ridge, named in honor of a slave once owned by Robert Henry. After Julie was freed, Henry built her a house at the foot of this mountain. Julie is buried beside Robert Henry.

Hester and Alexis are sometimes used as feminine first names but neither the Hester of Granville County, nor the Alexis of Gaston County, honor females. Hester was named for Henry M. Hester, who gave the land for the railroad right-of-way and station site in Granville. And Alexis was first called Alex's Cross Roads for a Mr. Alexander who was an early landowner in the community.

Some say the town of Sophia in Randolph County, settled before 1779 by Pennsylvanians of German ancestry, was named for Sophia, Electress of Hanover, mother of George I of England. Others say not true, that Sophia was named for local resident, Sophia Clement.

•••

There are disagreements, too, about the naming of Elizabeth City, in Pasquotank County, and Elizabethtown in Bladen County. One version is that the towns, both county seats, were named in honor of Queen Elizabeth.

Others say, absolutely not. Elizabeth City was named for Elizabeth Tooley, prosperous widow of Adam Tooley, who sold her plantation to the town commissioners when the town was built. The place was first incorporated in 1793 as Reading and changed to Elizabeth City in 1801.

Elizabethtown, it is said, was named for a girl whose last name isn't remembered. She was the sweetheart of Isaac Jones, who gave the land for the town site. The town was established in 1773, chartered in 1843, and incorporated in 1895.

Around 1745, Rufus Best owned a plantation in Greene County. He journeyed over to New Bern and met a young lady named Shine Oliver. Miss Oliver did not take a shine to Mr. Best but he certainly did to her. In spite of her rejection, he named his plantation Shine.

A later community in the area also was called Shine, although some say that the name came from a family named Shine who lived there. No matter, Shine community later became known as Rufe.

For Rufus Best perhaps? Still no matter, because the community no longer exists.

11
Honoring Him

Colonel Benjamin Cleaveland (and this spelling of the name is correct) could throw his weight around. Literally. All 300-plus pounds of it. His bulk didn't slow him down one whit during the Revolutionary War battles in which he fought, though. He became a hero at Kings Mountain.

Cleveland County (spelled without the *"a"*) is named for Big Ben. So is Ronda, the town in Wilkes County. Ben Cleaveland was a founder of Wilkes County—his land deed was the first recorded at the courthouse.

Roundabout was the name Cleaveland gave to his plantation on the Yadkin River. Maybe that name referred to a bend in the river. Or, as some say, Old Roundabout was Cleaveland's own nickname, which he enjoyed. Anyway, Ronda evolved from Roundabout.

Cleaveland, so a tale goes, once agreed to freeing a horse thief if the thief would cut off his own ears. The thief complied and Cleaveland sent the earless man on his way.

In later life, Cleaveland lost his plantation, ballooned to 450 pounds, and moved to South Carolina where he spent several years serving as a county judge. While on the bench, he sometimes snoozed to the drone of lawyers and witnesses. He paid a child to shoo flies off him and left instructions that he not be roused unless his snoring got too loud, or time came to pass judgment.

••

Mooresville in Iredell County was named for John Moore, a generous landowner who gave many acres for town growth. A man also generous in girth, he was said to have weighed more than 300 pounds. He died in 1877 at the age of fifty-four.

A story about early Mooresville maintains that when rain fell at the four corners of the town square, it was said to flow into four different rivers feeding the Atlantic Ocean.

Good old Daniel Boone, King of the Frontier. We love him. After all, he spent some good years with us.

Okay, so he wasn't born in North Carolina, but he lived for a time growing up in Davie County. And his parents, Squire and Sarah Boone, are buried near Mocksville (named for the Mock family who owned the landsite of the town).

About 1760, Daniel crossed the mountains through Deep Gap into new territory around the Watauga River and made a home in this section from 1760 until 1769. The town of Boone in Watauga County is named in his honor.

As is Boonville, in Yadkin County. Boonville was built where two Indian trails crossed. The East-West Trail was used mostly by the Cherokee, the North-South Trail by the Catawba. Dr. Nathan B. Dozier, in the late 1800s, was the local person who suggested the name Boonville, because Daniel Boone frequently had hunted and camped there. Boone supposedly slept in a favorite hollow poplar tree that stood near a large free-flowing spring.

The tree is gone but there is still a large spring a short distance west of the Boonville Baptist Church.

You *might* say that a couple of North Carolina place names resulted from a little Sir Isaac Newton fall-out. Newton Grove, in Sampson County, was named for the scientist. And Isaac Newton Wilson (named for Sir Isaac) was the inspiration for the town of Newton in Catawba County. Isaac Newton Wilson was a member of the 1842 General Assembly and introduced the bill creating Catawba County. Newton is Catawba's county seat.

John Thomas Spivey was a spiffy dresser. Nothing flashy, mind you, but consistently neat and complete. Black suit, white shirt, string tie, and black hat. It might have been a carry-over from his days working with the Tilghman Lumber Company.

Or was he a retired judge, as some people speculated? He had that manner about him, they said, pointing out Spivey's authoritative personality and the way he was always firm, yet fair, in his dealings with people.

He came to the area in Sampson County which now bears his name as a timber cruiser for the lumber company. When he retired in the 1920s, he bought a store and operated it for many years. His store stood in the northeast corner of what is now the crossroads community of Spivey's Corner, famous throughout the country for its annual hollering contest.

William D. Sylva was a young man from Denmark who passed through Jackson County in 1879 and left his name behind.

Sylva apparently was down on his luck when he knocked at the door of Judge Riley Cannon and asked for hospitality. He got that and more from Cannon, who gave him a place to stay and asked his neighbor, General E. R. Hampton, to give Sylva a job.

Hampton was glad to oblige. He owned a sawmill and was at that very time building a home. If Sylva continued to live at Cannon's, he could have a job until Hampton's house was finished.

Sylva stayed, worked hard, and won the friendship of nearly everyone who came to know him. He always had time to greet Hampton's little daughter, tease her a bit, and leave her smiling.

Sylva could have stayed on when Hampton's house was completed, but he had places yet to see, so he left. Not long thereafter, a post office was established at the sawmill site, and a search for a name began. Hampton's little daughter had the winning nomination. "Let's call it Sylva after William," she said.

William D. Sylva never returned to his namesake town but his daughter may have. In 1924, someone heard that Sylva was living in Cleburne, Texas, but nobody confirmed it. In 1951, when Jackson County was celebrating its 100th anniversary, the Sylva postmaster wrote Cleburne, Texas, inquiring about William Sylva. Sylva's daughter answered the inquiry.

William Sylva had seen enough by the time he reached Texas and settled there, his daughter said. He became a carpenter and contractor, married, had children, grandchildren, and was active in the community. Whether he ever knew that a town in North Carolina bore his name is not known.

A town in Orange County has carried the name of two men. It was incorporated as Venable in 1911, for Francis P. Venable (1845-1924), president of the University of North Carolina. Citizens changed the name in 1913 to Carrboro, in honor of Julian S. Carr, who established a textile mill there.

The town of Youngsville in Franklin County was incorporated in 1875 and named for prominent citizen John Young, who gave the land for the first railroad depot. But it turned out not to be easy to call the place Youngsville.

For twelve years the post office went by the name Pacific while the railroad station was called Youngsville. What confusion! Fortunately, most people living there had a sense of humor. They took to calling a part of town on one side of the railroad tracks Atlantic and the part on the other side Pacific.

Finally, maybe from sheer exhaustion, the name Youngsville won out.

The earliest settler of a community in McDowell County was Jack Parker. Small wonder, then, that it's called Jacktown.

12
Circumstances

For anyone who has lain awake nights wondering how Montgomery County's town of Abner got its name, relax. It was named for Abner.

The dilemma is, who was Abner?

There was Abner Lucas, one of the area's first settlers. Could have been named in his honor. If so, why wasn't it called Lucas?

There was "Old Man Abner," who hid out from the Confederate soldiers on the mountain that became known as Abner's Mountain.

And there was the school principal named Abner, but no-one seems to remember any other part of his name. His school in the vicinity existed sometime before the turn of the century.

We can't ask the real Abner to please stand up, so don't fret it.

Joe Balding was a driving force in getting a post office located on Meadow Fork Creek in Madison County. Nobody worked harder than he did to prove that the place needed its own identity and postal delivery. That's why it was fitting and proper that he select the new name.

"My goodness, Joe," his wife said. "Choosing a name is a big responsibility. You need to give it a lot of thought."

"I am, honey," said Joe.

"Maybe you ought to name it in honor of somebody, Joe," she said.

"I'm considering it, honey," said Joe.

"And Joe, it should be a short name that everybody can spell and understand right off," she said.

"I wouldn't have it any other way, honey," said Joe. And smiled.

That, they say, is how Joe got its name.

Poor Jonas Braswell. He froze to death against a rock on a mountain ridge in Burke County. Braswell, his wife, and a young woman were making a trip on foot across the mountain to a place called Pensacola. A harsh winter storm set in and try as they might, they couldn't get a fire going.

"I can't make it," Jonas told his wife. "You two go on and get outta here."

"Don't worry, Jonas," the women told him. "We'll find help and come back soon."

The women struggled across the rugged terrain in the blasting winds as quickly as they could. Their hearts leaped with hope when they met Avery County brothers, Jacob and William Carpenter, and the men went back to rescue Jonas. They brought him by horseback to their home.

Despite the rescue and all efforts to revive him, the old man did not survive. The mountain range where he huddled and breathed his last is called Jonas Ridge.

Most everyone agrees that Andrew J. Dunning played a part in naming the Bertie County town of Aulander. What isn't agreed on is, what part?

The original name of Aulander was Harman's Crossroads, because of several Harmans who lived there. Dunning was a Harman in-law, who owned some land in the Orlando, Florida, area. Now, Dunning enjoyed going back and forth to

Florida, figuring it was a nice place to visit but he didn't want to live there. He liked living at Harman's Crossroads. He also liked the name Orlando but didn't like the spelling.

So, when Harman's Crossroads needed a new name, Dunning suggested Orlando, but spelled the word with North Carolina creativity.

Another version is that Andrew J. Dunning, a prominent business man, named the town after himself, "Ol' Ander."

The Pitt County town of Grimesland had several names before settling on the name honoring Confederate General J. Bryan Grimes.

It was first known as Boyd's Ferry, then Mt. Calvert, then Nelsonville, before changing to Grimesland in 1887. (Part of the town is located on a portion of what was once 5,000 acres of Grimes' land.)

General Grimes survived the Civil War in spite of fighting in several of the bloodiest battles and having his horse shot from under him more than once.

Grimes was not as fortunate against an assassin's bullet on August 14th, 1880.

On that day, he stopped to water horses at Pitt County's Bear Creek. He had no way of knowing that death stood behind a tree in the person of William Parker, who shot him.

Parker, who was twice tried for the crime but not convicted, turned out to be his own worst enemy. Eleven years later, he got drunk in Little Washington and bragged of killing Grimes. He was found dead not long afterward. He had been lynched.

Some folks are so lucky that you'd want to carry them along to Vegas, if you were a mind to go. Except Otway Burns lived so long ago that Vegas wasn't even a twinkle in anybody's eye.

And it's Otway Burns, we're talking about. The towns

of Otway in Carteret County, and Burnsville in Yancey County are named for him. Which, of course, is a great honor, but it's not the aforementioned luck.

Burns had a lucky bout of rheumatism during the War of 1812. It caused him suffering but it saved his hide. He was laid up at home one day, when the British thought for sure they had him in their clutches.

Burns, you see, was the skillful maneuverer of the privateer ship *Snap Dragon* and had so aggravated the British that they offered a $50,000 reward for his capture. Trouble was, Burns wasn't on board the day the *Snap Dragon* was captured. He was home in bed with his rheumatic misery.

So, how come Easterner Burns has the town of Burnsville in the western part of the state named for him? It was for what Burns did long after the war, when he became a member of North Carolina's General Assembly. Burns strongly supported creating the new county of Yancey. Burnsville is the county seat.

Andrew Jackson, seventh President of the United States (1829-1837), is honored several times in North Carolina place names. There's Jackson County, to start with. Then, the town of Jackson, which is the county seat of Northhampton. And the Union County community of Jackson between Waxhaw Creek and Cane Creek, near Jackson's birthplace.

The county seat of Onslow County is Jacksonville, and named for "Old Hickory."

And Jackson Hill, a town in Davidson County. They say Jackson Hill got its name the day one of Andrew Jackson's strongest supporters raised a flagstaff here in celebration of Jackson's 1828 election to the presidency.

13
Faith and Religion

John Thomas Wyatt had little quarrying experience when he settled on rocky terrain in Rowan County and began his stone operation. He learned quickly and at one time shipped as many as five carloads of stone in a day. This was in a time when stone had to be hauled out in wagons, and it took about fifteen wagonloads to fill one rail car.

The stone quarry, which was the largest employer in the area in those early years, gave rise to the town of Faith. Wyatt was responsible for the town's name, as well.

Somebody asked Wyatt how he managed to accomplish so much considering his lack of experience. "I did it on faith," he said. "I had unbounded faith in the future of the community and myself."

Mt. Ulla Community in Rowan County was first called Woodgrove for the name of Captain Thomas Cowan's plantation. The Reverend A. Y. Lockridge, pastor of Back Creek Presbyterian Church, provided the later name. Lockridge selected "Mt." because of the rolling hills of the area. Biblically, "Ulla" is mentioned (descendant of Asher) in 1 Chronicles 7:39, "And the sons of Ulla, Arah, and Haniel, and Rezia."

Lockridge was a scholar and may have chosen Ulla from other sources: the river of that name in Spain, or a place in Scotland (many settlers of the area were from Scotland), or an Irish village by the name of Oola, or even from a term used in Scandinavian mythology.

Dr. Gideon Monroe Roberts founded the town of Mount Olive in Wayne County, and he, with settlers William F. Pollock and Benjamin Oliver (a son of a Baptist minister) named the town for the biblical Mount of Olives.

Mount Gilead, a town in Montgomery County, was named for the biblical mountain mentioned in Genesis 31: 21,25.

Mount Carmel Community in Vance County took the name of a local church named for the biblical mountain in Palestine where Elijah called down fire from heaven.

Mount Pisgah is on the Buncombe-Haywood county line and the view from its top includes areas in North Carolina, South Carolina, Georgia, Tennessee, and Virginia. This Mount Pisgah bears the name of the biblical mountain where Moses saw the Promised Land.

Early settlers named the McDowell County community of Nebo for Mt. Nebo of the Bible. From Deuteronomy 34:1, "And Moses went up from the plains of Moab unto the mountain of Nebo, to the top of Pisgah, that is over against Jericho."

Jericho is the name of a community in Caswell County. Another Jericho community is in Davie County and was named for the Jericho Church of Christ established there in 1872. The Jericho community which once existed in Wayne County was destroyed by Union forces during the battle of Whitehall, December 16th, 1862. (The site of this Jericho is now part of the corporate limits of Seven Springs.)

Jerusalem Township is in Davie County. Nash County's community of Samaria was named for the Samaria Baptist Church. Bethel (*house of God*) communities and towns exist in Caswell, Haywood, Hoke, Perquimans, Pitt, Watauga, and Wayne Counties. Bethel Hill is in Person County.

Bethany Community, in Davidson County, was first called Fredericktown by its German settlers, then for some unrecalled reason we can only imagine, became known as Possumtown. It changed its name in 1861 to Bethany, because of Bethany Church being built there. There is also a Bethany Community in Rockingham County, and the Bethany Community in Iredell County got its name from the Bethany Presbyterian Church organized there in 1775.

Presumably, the Bethlehem Communities—one in Alexander County, another in Hertford, were named for Bethlehem, Jordan, the birthplace of Jesus. (Redland in Davie County was once known as Bethlehem for Bethlehem Methodist Church.)

Reverend Thomas Price named Wake County's Nazareth for the town in the Bible first mentioned in the New Testament, but which actually predates historic times. A Hoke County town is named Antioch, possibly for the city of Antioch (in Turkey), an early center of Christianity.

Surry County's Siloam was named for the Old Siloam Methodist Church. The biblical pool of Siloam, where a blind man bathed his eyes in the waters and regained his sight, was the inspiration for the church's name.

Ararat Community in Surry County is named for the

Ararat River, named for the biblical Mount Ararat. Genesis 8:4: "And the ark rested in the seventh month, on the seventeenth day of the month, upon the mountains of Ararat."

Yarber Williams, a young businessman in 1886, is said to have named the village of Vashti in Alexander County. Williams had interests in sawmilling and building and other residents asked him to put a name to the village. He decided on Vashti, which was the name of a local woman, who likely was named after the biblical Vashti.

You remember Vashti. According to the Bible, Esther 1:1-19, Vashti was a beautiful queen, wife of King Ahasuerus. One day the king and some of his court were partying, and the king, his head giddy from too much wine, decided he wanted to show off his beautiful wife.

Ahasuerus sent servants to bring Vashti to him, but she refused to go to the king. This embarrassed Ahasuerus and infuriated him. No-one, let alone his wife, disobeyed the king. He banished Vashti from the throne.

Bishop Levi Silliman Ives, Episcopal Diocese, named Watauga County's Valle Crucis in 1842. Valle Crucis is Latin for "Valley of the Cross," which is the image Ives saw as he looked down into the valley from mountain heights above. He saw a cross-shaped cloud of fog arising from streams flowing below. Dutch Creek, running north and south to form the trunk of the cross, with Valley Creek on the west, and Charles Creek on the east, forming the arms.

Montgomery County's Ophir, settled in the late 1700s, got its name because of gold deposits there. The deposits reminded settlers of the biblical land where Solomon got gold for his temple.

The Christian Light Community in Harnett County

took its name from Christian Light Church organized in 1886 with Rev. George Underwood as first pastor. Community resident Abe Arnold is credited with the name. "Let all church members and people of the community strive to be "lights for Christ," Arnold said.

Also in Harnett County, in Buckhorn Township, is the Cokesbury Community. First known as Chalk Level in the 1700s, the community changed its name to honor the Cokesbury United Methodist Church established in 1836. (This church is the oldest Methodist congregation in Harnett County.)

Vance County's community of Cokesbury is at the head of Rocky Branch. The Cokesbury name itself is a combination of the last names of two Methodist bishops: Thomas Coke (1747-1814) and Francis Asbury (1745-1816).

There are Asbury communities in Montgomery, Stokes, and Wake Counties, with Wake County's Asbury being named by the community's founder, Calvin Bridgers, for Asbury, England.

Mecklenburg County's Providence grew around the Providence Presbyterian Church, organized in 1767. Caswell County also has a Providence community, as do Granville and McDowell Counties. And Providence Townships are in Pasquotank, Randolph, and Rowan. The Rowan township supposedly got its name because an act of providence helped General Nathanael Greene cross the Yadkin River in 1781 to escape Cornwallis.

The place names of Sharon, Arba, Zion, Zionville, Bishop's Cross, and many others likely reflect religious influence.

If you travel to western Davidson County, you can find the community of Churchland.

• • •

Angel Mountain, in Macon County, between Bryson Branch and Moore Creek, seemingly hovers over the countryside.

And yes, we have Eden. Since 1967 in Rockingham County, when the towns of Leaksville, Draper, and Spray merged. The new town was named for the Land of Eden, the former 20,000-acre estate of William Byrd (1674-1744). Byrd loved the beauty of his lands and thought not even Eden could be lovelier. The estate was along the Dan River in Rockingham County.

14
Love and Marriage

While traveling in Sampson County, you may move over ground included in the Sharecake area and never even know it. Boundaries of Sharecake are, after all, liberally interpreted. If you insist on geographical specifications, consider that Sharecake may extend northward to Craddock Swamp, westward to Daughtry Bridge on Big Coharie, and eastward to the old Raleigh Road, now US 701.

It was in the late 1870s that Sharecake got its name. A wedding, and invitations—or lack of them—started it all.

A lovely young lady, who shall remain nameless, was getting married. As all brides do, she longed for the perfect wedding. Which meant, of course, scads of happy people milling around, focusing their unwavering and *quiet* attention on the bride and groom.

It did *not* mean inviting more guests than could be gracefully served at the reception, or three known pranksters. Good heavens, no telling what would happen if she invited those boys. They'd be as likely to stand up and sing some roguish song during the ceremony, as not.

Well, maybe they would have or maybe they wouldn't have. Anyway, the three known pranksters were ticked off about not being invited, and they decided then and there they would do *something*.

On the day of the wedding, the three friends picked up a nearby farm worker who went along because he was glad to be included. They went to the bride's home where the wedding festivities were in full swing. Guests were coming and going in a steady stream. There was laughter, clinking of glasses, sweet music drifting in the air.

The foursome headed straight for the locked smokehouse where they knew the wedding refreshments were stored. They pried apart smokehouse logs and put the small, wiry farm worker inside to hand out the food. They ate until stuffed, and took the rest and scattered it on the ground. Then they lowered the log and left the worker trapped inside.

On the smokehouse door, they left a note. "If after dancing and singing, you folks are hungry, eat this farmhand."

Of course, the bride and groom were not amused, but some who had not been invited to the wedding, were. "Wouldn't have happened if they'd been willing to share the cake," they said and snickered in that mean way jealousy prompts. Others asked as they met up, "Were you invited to share cake?" It got to be where the whole place was being called that.

The bride and groom? Maybe they didn't have the chance to share their cake, but we've heard they shared many happy years together.

Fuquay-Varina, in Wake County, began as two separate communities. Fuquay (known by Indians as Sippihaw) was there first and called Fuquay Springs by the time it was incorporated in 1909. Frenchman William Fuquay allegedly paid only fifty cents for 1,000 acres to start the settlement. His grandson, David Crockett Fuquay, found a strong mineral spring on the land, and David's son, Stephen, developed the land into a health resort. (Fuquay Springs was named for David Crockett Fuquay.)

It's the "Varina" part of the name that offers a love

story. J. D. Ballentine, who operated a private school in the community, left and joined the Confederate Army at the beginning of the War Between The States. Young women back home set about doing what they could to cheer the boys who went to war. The girls selected pen pals and wrote often to the boys at the front.

Ballentine was a popular young man and soon had several female pen pals. One wrote extremely interesting letters and Ballentine found himself falling in love with her. One problem, though. He didn't know who she was. She signed her name "Varina" but admitted that this was not her real name.

Was Varina shy or did she wisely allow an air of mystery to accompany her words?

After the war, Ballentine went in search of Varina and found her. She was Virginia Avery but before long, she was Virginia Avery Ballentine. Ballentine became the first postmaster and named the post office Varina.

There are those who say, though, that Varina was named for Varina Davis, wife of Confederate President Jefferson Davis. Fuquay Springs and Varina merged in 1963 to become one town.

When the railroad came to a Catawba County village, Southern Railroad officials advised residents it was time to settle on a name. Its first name had been "Charlotte Crossing," but that had not lasted long before being shortened to Crossing to avoid confusion with the town of Charlotte. Then the place was known briefly as Setzer's Depot. Was that the official name citizens wanted? No, it wasn't, but what to choose?

Frank Cannon, who was with the railroad, had an idea. He thought of a pleasant-sounding one-word name, which had a first syllable from the name of the girl he was dating—Clara Sigmon. (He didn't figure the name honor would hurt him any in the romance department, either.) The last syllable of the name would be "mount" or "mont" because the village site, viewed from certain angles, looked as if it could be on a mountain.

The name was a winner. Claremont had an official name on August 8th, 1892. It's highly possible that Frank Cannon won the heart of Clara Sigmon, too.

Lucama, in Wilson County, is the combination of girls' names. The story is that Josephus Daniels, who grew up in Wilson County, named the town (around 1883) honoring three young ladies. Sources disagree on the girls' last name (which could have been Borden) and their relationship with Daniels. Some say he was seeing all three girls romantically, and others say the girls were simply family friends.

There is little disagreement, though, that the girls' first names were: Lucy, Carrie, and Mary. And that Lucama is the name derived from using the first two letters of each girl's name.

Iredell County has a town called Love Valley. It's a western town, complete with wooden structures and sidewalks, and the creation of entrepreneur Andy Barker, who founded the town in the 1960s. Certainly, those who love horses are right at home there, and weddings have taken place in Love Valley.

Oh, ye spinster ladies, don't get excited upon hearing of Bachelor Creek. The Bachelor Creek in Jones County was named for Edward Batchelor who was spoken for long ago. And the Bachelor Creek in Randolph County got its name because of a wild stallion who once roamed the area. People called the animal "the bachelor" since he was always alone.

Now, there's a Husbands Creek in Caldwell County, but be still, romance-hungry hearts. It was named for early settler, Veazey Husband.

And it's sad to tell you that the names of Sugar Grove,

Sugar Hill, and Sugar Hollow, in Watauga, McDowell, and Yancey Counties, respectively, have absolutely nothing to do with smack, smack, kissy-face. They were all named for sugar maple trees growing nearby.

It could be just as well. Listen to what Sir William Byrd, American Colonial writer and official, wrote in his journal (later published in his *History of the Dividing Line*) about Rockingham County's Matrimony Creek. In Sir William's own words:

"About Four miles beyond the River Irvin we forded Matrimony Creek, call'd so by an unfortunate marry'd man because it was exceedingly noisy and impetuous."

Well, Sir William must have looked at what he had written and with an eye towards later publication, added:

"However, tho's the Stream was clamorous, yet, like those Women who make themselves plainest heard, it was likewise clear and unsully'd."

Smart fellow, that William.

15
Big City Relatives

There are North Carolinians who can go over to Dallas for lunch and be home in time for an afternoon nap. They won't locate TV's South Fork Ranch, though.

This Dallas is in the center of Gaston County and was the original county seat from 1846 until 1909 when Gastonia assumed that role. Dallas, Texas, didn't inspire the name, but George M. Dallas, who was vice-president of the United States at the time, did. Vice-president Dallas was a Democrat who served under James K. Polk.

Denver is a hop, skip, and jump away to some of us, situated as it is in northeastern Lincoln County. When settled, around 1770, it was called Dry Pond by some folks with a sense of humor—a nearby area was swampy. In 1873, school principal, D. Matt Thompson suggested naming Dry Pond for the Colorado city, since Colorado was being considered for admission to the union.

Professor Thompson went on to become superintendent of schools in Statesville, Iredell County, and for many years a high school (later a junior high) in Statesville carried his name. That building is now part of Mitchell College's Continuing Education campus.

If you're traveling on US Highway 19E between Plumtree and Cranberry in Avery County near the Tennessee border, stop in Minneapolis. (You're nowhere near Saint Paul, but in Robeson County you'll find St. Pauls.) Years ago, asbestos was mined in Minneapolis, but now it is beautiful country with a small-place cozy feeling. Settlers with Minnesota roots named the place Minneapolis in 1892.

Columbus is the county seat of Polk County and isn't nearly as large as Columbus, Ohio, or Columbus, Georgia. It wasn't named for either. Columbus honors Dr. Columbus Mills, a member of the General Assembly that created Polk County in 1855.

North Carolina's Columbia is the county seat of Tyrrell County, in an area once the home of King Blunt, a Tuscaroran chief who was friendly with the English. The place was first a trading post known as Shallops Landing. Then, around 1680, explorers Captain Thomas Miller and Col. Joshua Tarkenton were so taken with the beauty of the countryside, they named it Heart's Delight. Around 1800, the town was called Elizabeth but it was renamed in 1810. This time the town honored Christopher Columbus. South Carolina's Columbia is larger, the capital of the state, and the seat of Richland County.

Alas, poor Richmond no longer exists. Our North Carolina version, that is. It was once the county seat of Surry (1774-1789) but a cyclone destroyed Richmond in 1830. Richmond, Virginia, however, is reportedly alive and well.

By the time you get to Phoenix, you'll be in Brunswick County. This Phoenix got its first post office in June, 1873. The name comes from the ancient legend of a bird, the phoenix, which when it had reached 500 years of age, burned itself on a pyre. From the ashes, another phoenix arose. The phoenix is widely used as a symbol of death and resurrection in literature.

• • •

North Carolina's Washington is the county seat of Beaufort County. Most North Carolinians believe that of this nation's 400-plus cities and towns named for George Washington, this town was the first.

The earliest recorded mention of the town as Washington was in an order of the council of safety at Halifax, dated October 1, 1776. Col. James Bonner, who was a founder of the town and a friend of Washington's, suggested the name. Before Washington, the name had been Forks of the Tar.

We have our own Cleveland in Rowan County, but it was first known as Third Creek. In 1887, the town changed its name to honor U. S. President Grover Cleveland. Cleveland was our 22nd and our 24th president.

Not that it has one thing to do with the place name, but Grover Cleveland is the only president to have been married in the White House.

In Cleveland County, we have the town of Waco, settled around 1857 and named by George W. Hendrick for Waco, Texas. The Pender County community of Honolulu was named for Honolulu, Hawaii.

Gloucester is a city in Massachusetts with a North Carolina namesake. Gloucester, North Carolina, settled about 1800, is in Carteret County.

Another North Carolina Gloucester was planned in the 1750's. Plans were for this Gloucester to be in Anson County on fifty acres owned by John Jenkins on the south side of the Pee Dee River. What happened to the town's authorization? The answer is lost in time, but the town never developed.

Ever been to Milwaukee? We're not talking Wisconsin. We're talking the North Carolina place in Northhampton

County. When settled around 1889, it was called Bethany.

Later on when the railroad came, Hezekiah Lasker, a railroad conductor who had migrated from Wisconsin, suggested the new place name. There were already several Bethanys around this state, Lasker said, and Milwaukee had a nice sound to it.

Selma in Johnston County was first known as Mitchiner's Railroad Station for John Mitchiner, local resident. In 1873, because an owner of land around the station refused to sell it so the place could develop commercially, Henry Webb, president of the North Carolina Railway, approved the moving of the station to a new location.

This is the alleged scientific, geographically accurate method used to determine the new location. They loaded a small railway station house onto a flat rail car and gave it a hefty shove to the east. When the flat car stopped about a mile away, that place became the new station and town site.

The movers and shakers involved in this event already had a new name picked out: Selma, for the city in Alabama.

If you're thinking any one of the several North Carolina places named Jackson is named for Jackson, Mississippi, you're wrong. Andrew Jackson, more likely.

Looking for a recording contract? Try Nashville, Tennessee. For the sweet music of southern living, try Nashville, North Carolina, the town and county seat of Nash County. Nashville is named for General Francis Nash (1742-77), Revolutionary officer from Hillsborough, who died a hero's death during the Battle of Germantown.

Long Beach, California, and Long Beach, North Carolina (Brunswick County) have long beaches in common, but neither was named for the other.

16
Dreams, Hopes, and Feelings

We all crave a little of it from time to time. Relief, that is, the easing of tensions, pain, anxiety, and burdens. Maybe that's why the patent medicine called Hart's Relief was a popular product at a store in Yancey County a long time ago. Of course, the product's highly alcoholic content may have boosted popularity with a few consumers.

This particular store was in the gorge of the Toe River. It just happened that the need for a place name coincided with peak popularity of Hart's Relief. Naming the place Relief was the overwhelming choice.

"It sure is a burden picking out a name for a place, but somebody's got to do it," Joshua Lawrence Bowden may have remarked to his wife in the late 1800's. The Bowdens lived in Franklin County and were owners of their community's general store.

Mr. and Mrs. Bowden hadn't asked for the task of picking out a post office and community name. Other folks had asked them to, and the Bowdens were obliging people. Besides, Mrs. Bowden was going to be the first postmaster.

In the beginning, the couple considered naming the place for themselves, since that seemed simplest. People already referred to a trip to the store as going over to Bowden.

But there was already an established town in the eastern part of the state named Bowden, so no need to confuse everybody. Mrs. Bowden expressed the opinion that the place needed a name having meaning for everyone. "I, for one, believe in justice for all," she said.

"My dear, you've hit upon the name," Mr. Bowden said (or words to that effect). "Let's call it Justice."

When the Cabin Creek Post Office in Montgomery County needed a name change in 1885, three local merchants put their heads together to decide what it should be. "Ours will be a town where frankness and sincerity will prevail," they predicted. "So, let's call the place Candor."

The less poetic version of this name origin is that a former resident of Candor, New York, wanted to honor his previous home.

In 1900, William Plemmons wanted a post office established on Upper Spring Creek in Madison County. He wrote to the Post Office Department and politely asked for one, and, incidentally, for a job. "I trust that I will have the luck of becoming postmaster of this community," Plemmons wrote.

Plemmons hit the jackpot. The Department granted not one, but two post offices on Spring Creek, and borrowing from the wording of Plemmons' request, approved Trust as the name of one post office and Luck for the other. Fittingly, Plemmons became the postmaster of Luck.

Mount Mourne is one of Iredell County's oldest towns and before the Revolution a carriage maker had a shop there. Near the carriage shop stood a small hill which was often used for slave auctions. The auctions were a time of grief for persons being sold and their families. Mournful cries filled the air and the hill became known as "Mount Mourn." Another version for the Mount Mourne name is that settler Rufus Reid named his fine home, Mount Mourne, for the mountain in Ireland and that the town is named for Reid's home.

• • •

Hope springs eternal...at least that's what settlers desired when they made their homes near a bountifully flowing spring in Nash County. They hoped the spring would flow forever for their use and named the place Spring Hope.

In the 1880s a California entrepreneur visited a site in Chatham County and fell in love with a dream. His dream involved worms, trees and beautiful cloth. The man was certain that the climate and terrain he found were suitable for growing the white mulberry tree (*Morus multicaulis*).

He planted a grove of the trees and after some months when they took growth, he brought in silkworms to feed on the mulberry leaves. If things went well, the silkworms would flourish and spin their cocoons of silken strands. The lustrous fabric is made from those strands.

But he had misjudged growing conditions for the trees. They needed more moisture than the climate provided and grew poorly. In turn, the silkworms did not reproduce as expected, and the venture failed.

In the 1950's the remains of the mulberry orchard were cleared away. The man's name has been forgotten by most but a reminder of his dream remains in the name of the town, Silk Hope.

New Hope is the name of a community in Franklin County. Also, the name for communities in Iredell, Randolph, Wayne, and Wilson Counties. New Hope symbolizes the optimistic outlook of early settlers.

Who doesn't wish to live in concord and be in harmony with our fellow man? We can in North Carolina.

Mosey on down to Cabarrus County. Or to Duplin, Person, Sampson, or Yancey Counties, where you can live in communities named Concord. The larger Concord is a city in Cabarrus.

Cabarrus County's Concord incorporated in 1798 and the name came from the ability of two factions to agree amicably on the town's location. Scotch settlers in the western area and German settlers in the eastern portion each wanted the new county courthouse. After several heated discussions, they compromised on a half-way site and named the place Concord.

For congenial living, visit northeastern Iredell County where you'll find the town of Harmony. The name comes from the Harmony Hill Camp Meetings held here during the middle 1800s. The first records of the meetings show that people gathered for a two-week preaching event each October. People came from miles around and camped in crude shelters. It was a wonderful visiting and spiritually uplifting occasion for them and they experienced harmony. The place incorporated in 1874 as Harmony Hill Camp Ground, but in 1927 the name changed simply to Harmony.

For a cheerful boost, visit two places with sunny names. Try Sunburst community in Haywood County. Sunburst got its name because the sun rises quickly from behind a mountain range, giving a sudden and glorious glow to the land.

Then there's Sunshine, a community in Rutherford County. Sometime before 1881, J. W. Biggerstaff had a general store there. He got to know well the nature of the place, noting each day how Cherry Mountain shaded his store in the early morning while on the mountain top sunshine reigned.

Biggerstaff chose to think sunny thoughts. "I'm calling this place Sunshine," he said, and he did.

Part III

Animal, Vegetable, and Mineral

17
Anatomically Speaking

Could be that you've traveled around North Carolina, asked directions from time to time, and heard something like this: "Go on straight till you get to Finger..." or "The house you're looking for is the second one on the right past Brokeleg Branch..." or "That fellow lives over in Black Ankle."

It's enough to make a person think that North Carolinians have a thing about anatomy.

Listen, we've got good reason for those names. And if we don't recall the reason, we can always make one up.

For instance, we've got three Black Ankle communities—one in Montgomery County, one in Randolph, and the other in Robeson. Each has a perfectly good reason—or two—for the name.

One version of the Montgomery County's Black Ankle is that a long time ago an eligible bachelor in the area took himself off to Pembroke and brought back a lovely Indian wife. This ticked off the ignored spinster ladies of the community so much they were beside themselves to find fault with her.

Try as they might, though, they couldn't find anything wrong with the new wife. She cooked up the tastiest dishes for her husband, hung the cleanest wash on the line, and didn't as much as blink a flirting eyelash at any man in the community.

But envy will find a speaking way most times. "Well," sniffed the spinsters, "she may be pretty and all that, but she's got this dark skin—bound to have black ankles."

Likely, the more accurate version for the name is this. There once was a working gold mine in the area and many men went down the mine shaft to work each day. Eventually the mine began filling with water and miners standing in dark mud oozing above their boot tops carried home mud caked on their feet and lower limbs—and most certainly, black ankles.

Randolph County's Black Ankle got its derisive nickname during Prohibition because of bootleggers. Supposedly moonshiners had some king-sized stills here and started large fires when the stills were running so law officers couldn't find the locations.

Anyone walking through the ashes got black ankles.

Robeson County's fertile soil prompted its Black Ankle name. Farmers plowing on foot through the rich soil got its blackness on their feet and ankles.

Now the ankle bone connects to the leg bone...but not to Brokeleg Branch which rises in Cherokee County and flows south into Gipp Creek.

Some say the branch got its name because of a little boy who slipped away from home to play in the branch, fell in and broke a leg.

Finger community in Stanly County is named for a family by that name who helped settle the area. Thumb Swamp in Bladen County had to do more with its geographical positioning than the short, thick digit of the hand.

Vein Mountain community in McDowell County is called that because of gold veins running through the mountain—not for the blood-carrying network.

There is a Blood Camp Ridge, though, in Avery County. It's where Billy Davis cut his foot a long time ago. And a Blood Creek over in Wilkes County. And there's a story about how Bloodrun Creek in Chatham County got that name:

During the Revolutionary War, a small group of Whigs and Tories fought a furious and bloody skirmish there. Both sides wanted to keep their losses secret, so they buried their dead quickly and privately. One of the burial places was near this creek and the survivors named the creek as a reminder of those who shed their blood in the struggle.

Bloody Rock is in Macon County, near Cullasaja. Sometimes a blood-colored liquid seeps from the rock which, if you believe the legend, is where one young man killed another over the love of a local girl.

Back Bay, Back Landing, all the Back Creeks, Back Lake, Back Sound, Back Swamps, and Back Creek Mountain, have to do with locations—forget about spinal cords. No fewer than twelve counties use "back" in a place name in some way.

It's probably a geographical thing, too, with Swain County's Big Head Branch, which flows southeast into Straight Fork. The same goes for Gum Neck community in Tyrrell County—likely the name comes from the gum tree and the place's situation on a canal, having nothing to do at all with the bodily part the head rests on.

Back in the 1870's, C. M. Tysor suggested Erect for his community's new post office in Randolph County. The name was to honor Tysor's neighbor, Tom Bray, who was not only a man of upstanding character but who had excellent posture. The name won approval.

Brrrrr. Bone Valley is in Swain County. An early settler was the first to call the place that after he found the bleached bones of his lost cattle scattered there.

Which brings us to Coldass Creek in Caldwell County. Oh sure, modern day sissies call it Cold Water Creek, but not everybody has forgotten that descriptive original name.

The same story accounts for the naming of Caldwell's Pinch Gut Creek, too.

Once upon a time, two hunters set out together to try their luck in some unfamiliar and unnamed territory. They began by following a stream to where it forked.

There, they talked about which fork to take and decided that each would take one and meet back at the end of the day. And for future reference, they agreed to name the forks after they returned—some appropriate name, they said, according to how they felt about the streams.

One man carried the food and the other sleeping equipment. Since they planned to meet later, there seemed no need to change that arrangement.

But as plans frequently do, this one miscarried. Each man lost his way and had to spend the night alone in the wilderness. By the time they struggled back to their meeting place the next day, the two hunters were not happy campers.

"This is Coldass Creek," declared the fellow who had carried only the food with him.

"And let this other miserable creek be known from here on out as Pinch Gut," grumbled the hunter who had slept well but hadn't eaten since the day before.

Of course, there's another version of how Pinch Gut Creek (or Branch, some call it) in Stokes County got its name. It has to do with the time Indians depended heavily on the creek for fish—a major source of their food supply.

A severe drought came and dried up the creek. Without fish, the people went hungry and felt "gut pinching." Most moved away to find better fishing and hunting.

If you think the name of Defeat Branch in Swain County has something to do with combat, you are wrong. It was named after a hunter got his shoes burned up in a campfire while he dozed away here during a snowstorm.

• • •

Footsville, in Yadkin County, used to be called Footville. The only explanation we've heard is that a fellow named "Foote" once lived there.

Anyway, until we hear something definite, we'll stand on that account.

18
Savory Syllables

Traveling in North Carolina can make your mouth water. Nothing subliminal, either, about those signs announcing that you're in or approaching Cranberry, Turkey, or Riceville. Or Ramp Cove or Lemon Springs or Salmon Creek. Or Dillsboro, Tater Hill, or Big Kitchens. Or Table Rock, for that matter. Makes you think of eating with a taste of home.

To tell the truth, not all North Carolina place names that sound food related are.

Take Dills Branch in Jackson County. That name hasn't the slightest connection with pickles or bread or the aromatic seed from the parsley plant family. The stream is named for Allen B. Dills who lived nearby.

The same goes for Dillsboro, also in Jackson County, except this town got its name from town founder, William A. Dills, who was a member of the General Assembly, 1889-91. The first post office here, known as Cowee Tunnel, was in Dills' home and Mrs. Dills was postmaster.

Salmon Creek will disappoint if you expect those big fish swimming. There's not a salmon in the entire length of this Bertie County Creek. The name probably came from an early settler whose name may have been Salmon or sounded like it.

• • •

There are no lemons in the Lemon Springs. Minerals, yes. Puckery fruit, no. In 1890, when the railway came to this Lee County area, the railway station took the name of Lemon Springs, because of nearby natural springs owned by a family named Lemon, or Lemmon. Locals appreciated the mineral water as a healthful tonic and the springs' site as a lovely picnic area.

It's rather embarrassing since the subject of food place names *has* been mentioned—but there is no barbecue in Barbecue Swamp. Red Neill McNeill, about 1750, named this Harnett County marsh. He saw early morning mists from the swamp and they reminded him of smoke rising from barbecue pits he had seen in the West Indies.

If you're looking for that ground corn staple of southern cooking, hominy grits, you may not find it on Hominy Creek, which rises in Haywood County and flows into Buncombe where it enters the French Broad River. At one time you could have found hominy there, according to local legend:
A South Carolina hunting party, before the Revolution, camped by this creek on the first night of their trip and cooked themselves up a big pot of hominy for supper.
Records dating back to 1764 show a Hominy Swamp in Wilson County. Some think the name came from a hominy mill operated on the waters of the swamp.

The first white settler in the Bull Creek area of Buncombe County was Joseph Rice, who has the dubious distinction of killing the last buffalo seen in the county. The community of Riceville in the county is named for the Rice family.

Butters Community in Bladen County got its name from the Butters Lumber Company that was here.

• • •

Yes, there are ramps in Cherokee County's Ramp Cove, much to the delight of those who savor this wild leek. And if you're lucky, and there in the right season, you'll find wild cranberries in Avery County's Cranberry. Perhaps you'll also find wild cranberries along the Cranberry Creeks in Avery, Ashe, Jackson, Watauga, and Yadkin. And huckleberries at Huckleberry Springs in Durham County. Most certainly, there are figs in Ashe County's community named Fig.

Wintergreen makes delicious mountain tea. This herb grows plentifully along Mountain Tea Branch in Transylvania County.

Northhampton County's Gumberry was settled about 1882 and likely named for a tree fruit found there and described by the early explorer, John Lawson. Lawson thought the tree was a kind of black gum and told of Indians using the berries in making soup and cooking peas and beans.

In Brunswick County an onion-like plant, the shallot, grows locally. The plant may account for the Shallotte name of the river and for the town located on the river. Some disagree and say that early settlers called the place Charlotte and Shallotte is a corruption of that name. The town was earlier called Shelote.

Once there was a boarding house in Cherokee County whose chief cook was not known as a great biscuit maker. Seems the cook had this thing about leaving those doughy wads in the oven long enough to cook through. Diners got to poking fun about eating "raw dough" over at the boarding house, and the on-going joke led to the community name of Rhodo.

Tater Hill (although some of the more fastidious call this Potato Hill) is a peak on Rich Mountain in Watauga County.

It got its name because the shape resembles a potato storage hill.

During the 1930's, a McDowell County community grew great numbers of sweet potatoes to sell to the W. P. A. Program. The potatoes were fire-cured and in much demand because of their excellent flavor. The community is still known as Tatertown.

If you travel to Turkey in Sampson County and actually see a turkey roaming about, don't get excited. The bird is probably an escapee from a turkey farm. In earlier days, though, wild turkeys lived in the area and were in plentiful supply along Turkey Creek, which runs along the northern borders of the town. In 1887, the Wilmington and Weldon Railroad built a branch line between Warsaw and Clinton, and named the depot Turkey.

It might seem natural to travel from Turkey to Thanksgiving (community, that is) all in the same county, but Thanksgiving Community is in Johnston County. It was named for a Baptist Church founded on the site in 1899.

What about Turkey Otter Creek in McDowell County? Are there turkeys and otters there today? Maybe. The name came from long ago and is not so factually documented, but the story goes something like this:

Back in the early days, a settler and his wife moved to a sparsely settled area of McDowell County. They loved the beauty of the mountain wilderness but the settler knew that a large supply of the family's food would need to come from his success as a hunter and trapper. He began immediately to set traps along a busy little creek and to take longer trips away from the cabin to hunt.

He was having little luck with his traps or gun, and he and his wife were having second thoughts about having made the move. One morning in mid-fall, the settler arose with a weary heart and talked quietly with his wife.

"I'm going out today and will go even further along the creek to see what I can find. If I have no luck, I think we need to plan on leaving before winter truly sets in."

His wife agreed and kissed him, wishing him a safe trip.

He checked the trap on the creek and found it empty. He began a long trek creek-side into the woods. Perhaps forty minutes later he came to a small clearing and there his heart leaped. Wild turkeys! He took careful aim and killed a fine gobbler.

The settler slung the turkey over one shoulder and started home. As he came to the trap which had been empty earlier, he saw that it now held a plump otter.

Of course, his wife was delighted to see him return with the turkey over one shoulder and the otter over the other. "I never wanted to leave this place, anyway," she said, "and now there's no need, living so near Turkey Otter Creek."

Travel North Carolina. Feast your eyes on the mountains of Big Kitchens Range in southeastern Clay County between Sassafras Branch and Holden Cove. Dine at Table Rock Mountain in Burke County. You'll be glad you brought along that well-filled goody basket.

19
Food and Drink

You'll scarcely find anyone nowadays in Halifax County who remembers Dumpling Town or the great dumpling cook-off. But this is the way it was:

The event was a long time ago, mind you, when cooking was a straight-from-scratch art form and fast food yet to be. In one area of the county lived a number of excellent cooks—all women, who prided themselves on dishing up one delicious specialty after another. Their husbands grew plump, gluttonous, and yes, downright spoiled. It actually got to where husbands put their heads together and connived to see how they could get their wives to turn out even more bountiful dishes. That conniving spawned the dumpling cooking contest.

"Honey, I bet you make the best chicken 'n dumplings of anybody in this place," said the fellow who started the whole thing, "except maybe for Ella Mae—Roger says he'd guarantee Ella's dumplings lighter and tastier than anybody's."

Now, this conversation, as preplanned by the men, went on in nearly all the homes, only the names got changed around. Well, the women got highly irritated with each other, thanks to those sneaky comments, so they said to their husbands, "Well, we'll just see about those dumplings! We're putting our dumplings where your mouths are, so there!" And they set a time for a great dumpling cook-off—husbands to be the judges of course, fair and square.

They set up long tables, like you'd have for a church's homecoming, out on the community's picnic grounds. The women arranged to do their dumpling cooking outside, in great iron pots over open fires. Men sat at tables, women donned aprons, and out in the warm spring air and sunshine, the cook-off began.

All kinds of dumplings were eligible. Meat dumplings were popular, with chicken being the favorite choice in that category. But fruit dumplings were being cooked, too. Prudy Lee and Iris Jane were both skillful with mouth-watering apple dumplings. A dozen or more ladies, with matching husbands, were involved in the cook-off.

One round of dumpling serving took place, then another, and another.... Men grinned, and forked, and licked their lips, and burped, and grinned some more, and sat waiting with forks in hand and sopped plates in front of them.

The women stirred, served, sweated, and waited for a decision. None came—only requests for more dumplings. Need more samples to judge from, the men said.

Finally, Irene decided that the men might not be getting fed up, but she was. "I'm smelling more here than apple dumpling breath," she muttered to Lucyanne who was wearily dishing up another round. "S'more like a rat, whaddya think?"

"You musta read my mind." answered Lucyanne.

Well, first one woman, then another, got to thinking and talking. Somebody commented that she thought her husband wanted to keep her barefoot, aproned, and elbow-deep in dumpling dough the rest of her life, and that remark brought nods from female heads all around.

The last comment heard was when one woman said she had a good mind to let her dumpling pot cool and then turn it upside down over some smirking male noggins at the picnic tables.

This is the last we know of the matter. Local inquiries

today bring averted glances and zipped lips. And wouldn't you know there's not a written word about who won the contest or further plans for the event? But for a long time thereafter that place was known as Dumpling Town.

While we're talking hungry, let's mention a place called Slay Bacon Branch in Graham County. That stream runs clearly and quickly through a pretty area. But the name? Visions of wild boar running alongside the stream? Hunting side meat on the hoof? Maybe, sometime, somewhere, but that's not why its called Slay Bacon.

An early settler in a log house by the stream loved bacon. No ifs and ands about it. For breakfast he had his wife slice the salt-cured meat as thin as she could get it without cutting herself—maybe eight slices, or ten—just for him. These she fried up crisp and he pressed them into half a dozen biscuits.

If he had to be away from home for awhile, he'd tuck a chunk of cooked bacon into his saddlebags with cornpone and a cooked sweet potato or two.

When he got home at night, just for variety's sake, he'd have thick-sliced bacon fried with onions or whatever fresh greens were on hand. He cut the evening meal's bacon slices himself. Said his wife never got the thickness just right.

It worked out all right for the couple, though. The wife didn't have to rack her brain about what to serve for meals, and neither had the foggiest notion about cholesterol.

The only problem was they might have heard some snickering from their neighbors. "That fellow slays bacon faster than his wife can fry it," neighbors gossiped to each other. They liked the couple, though, and would visit them. "Let's take a trip over to Slay Bacon Branch," somebody would say. Finally that name became so commonplace it stuck.

Speaking of frying pans, The Frying Pan in Tyrrell

County is a large body of water roughly shaped like one. But Fryingpan Gap on the Haywood-Transylvania County line got its name because of something other than shape. A generous soul left a frying pan at the campground there for others to use.

Macon County and Warren County both have Lickskillet communities. At least one of them got that name as a reminder to hunters not to leave unwashed cooking pans at campsites. If they did, animals were likely to lick those skillets clean.

And Meat Camp community in Watauga County got its name from Meat Camp Creek where early hunters camped, skinned, and salted down their game.

Tugwell stayed with the name of Tugwell until the early twentieth century. It was then the railroad established a stop at this place in Pitt County, bringing in more people to get acquainted and to learn what Tugwell had to offer.

Besides pleasant people and a sociable atmosphere, some passengers found a Tugwell store selling high-quality whiskey. Before long, the railroad stop at Tugwell became known as Toddy Station. Later, folks stopped using the Tugwell name and shortened the Toddy Station name to Toddy.

20
Pining

If you're averse to pine, better not hang around long in North Carolina, because *we love* pine.

The state tree is the pine. Our state toast declares right off: "Here's to the land of the long leaf pine...."

Pine trees provided our nickname: Tar Heels.

We relish the very word "pine." To us, it's a four-letter word with class. It works well with other words, as in Pine Hall and Pine Level. It's just as agreeable with combinations, as in Pinehurst and Pineville.

Back in 1914, the folks who lived in the Avery County community of Saginaw got the chance to rename their post office. They wanted something more descriptive or indicative of the area's image.

"I say we name it Pine," suggested one lady who was on the new-name committee. "We've got so many of those healthy-looking trees around here we oughta brag a little."

"Shoot, I say we call it Ola," said a young man who admired Ola Penland, the daughter of the local hotel-keeper. "She's sweet, nice, and pretty—her name would give the place the same image."

A natural-born negotiator spoke up. "Pineola doesn't sound half-bad to me," he said. It sounded good to the rest of the committee, too.

• • •

Henry Clark Bridgers, founder of the East Carolina Railway, named the town of Pinetops in Edgecombe County. The railway between Tarboro and Hookerton was completed in 1900, and Bridgers was on board for the first run.

"Seems like all I can see along here are pinetops," he observed.

The lay of the land, along with an abundance of needle-bearing trees, prompted early settlers of a town in Johnston County to name it Pine Level.

And wind murmuring through pines suggested Whispering Pines for a residential community in Moore County.

When the town of Vineland in Moore County had to change its name to avoid confusion with Vineland, New Jersey, townsfolk didn't get all ripped.

There they were, right on the edge of the longleaf pine belt. "So, forget about the Vineland name, Southern Pines describes us to a tree," residents told postal officials.

The citizens of Pinehurst, near Southern Pines and also in Moore County, liked the name for their town because of its location smack in the middle of a pine forest.

Isaac English once ran a tavern by the Toe River in Mitchell County. It was a popular gathering place, good for hearing news, swapping tales, and talking trades.

It was easy to find, too, because of the towering Carolina hemlock (commonly called spruce pine) growing nearby. Visiting took place beneath the tree even when the tavern was closed.

"See you up at the spruce pine," became so common to hear that Spruce Pine became the official name in 1907 when the town incorporated.

• • •

An early name for Buncombe County's Weaverville was Pine Cabin.

If you're still not convinced of the way we honor pine, consider Piney, Piney Green, Pine Ridge, Pinebluff, Pinelog, Pinedene....

And Pine Marsh, a tidal marsh island about a mile and a quarter long in northern Pamlico County.

Pine Grove is a community in Craven County. Piney Grove is a community in Caldwell County, as well as in Wayne County, and a township in Sampson.

Please don't forget Piney Creek, not one of the six of them.

How *did* we get the Tar Heel nickname? The same way the town of Tar Heel in Bladen County and Tarboro in Edgecombe County got theirs.

Choose from several versions. All agree that the longleaf pine forests of the coastal plains produce abundant amounts of turpentine, rosin and tar.

So that explains the "tar." But what about the "heel?"

Some say Tar Heel dates from the Civil War and was originally derogatory. "A brigade of North Carolinians...failed to hold a certain hill and were laughed at by the Mississippians for having forgotten to tar their heels that morning," so says the *Morris Dictionary of Word and Phrase Origins.*

Another version goes back to the Revolution and says the troops of British General Charles Cornwallis came up with the name after Carolina soldiers came from a river with tar sticking to their heels. (Tar was rafted downriver to port cities in barrels and often spilled along the waterfront, causing it to get on the feet of anybody who walked there.)

A favorite explanation is this:

During the Civil War, soldiers fording the Tar River (which rises in Person County) found their feet black with dumped tar. North Carolinians were known for standing firm on the front lines and admirers said the soldiers held fast to their posts because they had tar on their heels. After one of the fiercest battles, General Robert E. Lee said, "God bless the Tar Heel boys."

21
Leafy Havens

While we love our pines in North Carolina, we also cherish our deciduous trees and honor them with many place names.

Take hickory. We have a city by that name in Catawba County. It used to be called Hickory Tavern back in the days when the most visible building around was a log tavern, more than likely built from good, solid hickory trees. John Bradburn operated the tavern, and it was the most important stagecoach stop in early Catawba.

When the town incorporated in 1863, it chose the name Hickory Tavern. Ten years later, folks officially dropped Tavern for just plain Hickory.

Lone Hickory is a far smaller and less hectic place. In the nineteenth century, a single hickory tree stood in the middle of an intersection on Old Stage Road in Yadkin County. The road followed a former Indian trail which ran from Salem to Wilkesboro, and travelers camped on land near the intersection. Since this tree was the only hickory tree around, it became a directional guide. "Meet up with you at the lone hickory," travelers told each other.

In time, a permanent community developed near the hickory tree, and it seemed right for the place to become known as Lone Hickory.

Hickory also turns up in other place names around the

state. There's a Hickory community in Nash County, a passel of Hickory creeks and branches in different counties, several Hickory Coves and Hickory Gaps, and at least three Hickory Groves in Chatham, Mecklenburg, and Wake Counties.

Then there's poplar.

In Rowan County, not too far from St. Luke's Lutheran Church, a big yellow poplar once stood. We're talking long ago, because by the time the post office came with a place name mentioning the poplar tree, it was 1878.

The original community name was Forty-Four because it is forty-four miles from Charlotte and forty-four miles from Winston-Salem. But something that happened involving Revolutionary War hero Thomas Cowan, a bear, and a poplar tree accounts for Forty-Four being renamed Bear Poplar.

It was a beautiful day and the Cowans were in their horse-drawn carriage on the way to church. They were clipping along when the horses suddenly came to a whinnying, raring stop.

The carriage nearly turned over and Mrs. Cowan got all weepy.

"Shush, now sweetheart," said Capt. Cowan. "You're going to get your pretty face splotchy. I'll take a look and we'll be on our way."

The horses were still wild-eyed and trembling when he got out of the carriage, and he looked up into the branches of that big poplar and did a little shaking himself. A whopping black bear was staring right at him.

Capt. Cowan eased over to the horses, got hold of a harness and led them down the road past the tree. Then he climbed quickly back into the carriage.

"Nothing I can't take care of, honey," he said. "I'll drop you at church and join you later."

He did just that, but in the meantime, he went home, got his gun, and killed the bear. Turns out, the whole community was grateful for the bear's riddance, and the story became well-known about Thomas Cowan and the bear in the poplar tree.

Some bits of that poplar tree may still be around. A few years after he killed the bear, Cowan had the tree cut for shingles to be used on a mill at his farm, Woodgrove (on the Historic Register). A relative of Thomas Cowan, Miss Josie Graham, also kept a piece of the old yellow poplar tree.

Guess there's nothing left of the bear.

Indians enjoyed the shade and beauty of a grove of Chatham County oaks and held tribal celebrations there. That's why the place came to be called Merry Oaks.

A town in Johnston County is named Four Oaks. The economy class name-origin version is that the town took the name in 1889 because of four trees standing at the site of the new town's rail station.

Then there's the d-double-deluxe version of the Four Oaks name which goes like this: About the time the railway came to town, a railroad official, J. B. Exum, treed an opossum in an oak tree on the property of K. L. Barbour.

Barbour was a prominent man, the first to build a house in the town. The magnificent oak in which the 'possum took refuge stood in his front yard. Barbour agreed to let Exum and several other men try to get the 'possum from the tree. The 'possum wrapped its skinny tail around a limb and hung there like a stalactite, ignoring their efforts.

Frustrated, the men ended up cutting down the tree to get the possum. When Barbour's wife saw what they had done, she was furious.

Some weeks later, Barbour pointed out to his wife, who had complained with late evening headaches ever since the tree-cutting, that a sturdy sprout was arising from the trunk of the felled oak.

The good news continued. A second sprout appeared

beside the first, then a third, and finally, a fourth. Each grew strong and tall on the base of the broad trunk, until finally, four healthy new oaks stood where the old tree had been.

The Barbours were proud of their landmark, and other people in the area began to speak of being from the Four Oaks area. Four Oaks was the natural choice for the official name.

The name "Liberty Oak" given to a Randolph County tree may be why we have a town called Liberty. One story is that General Charles Cornwallis released some patriot prisoners near a big oak tree tree during the Revolution. Another is that in 1865 Union soldiers camped here under an oak tree while Sherman and Johnston talked at the nearby Bennett house about the surrender of the Confederate Army.

A third story is that Liberty's name is the same as that of John Leak's plantation. Leak settled here in 1807, and the town incorporated in 1889, using the plantation name.

While beautiful trees are abundant in and around Rutherford County's Forest City, they are not the reason for the name. In the first place, the original name was Burnt Chimney because James McArthur had the misfortune of having his home burn leaving only a standing chimney. McArthur did not rebuild on that site and for years the chimney stood as testimony to the ravages of the blaze.

The place was at a crossroads and it became the muster ground for the militia. By 1875 when a village had grown around the crossroads there, Burnt Chimney Academy was established to provide education for the young.

Burnt Chimney was changed to Forest City in 1887 to honor Forest Davis, a local lumber dealer.

Wilson County's Elm City *was* named for elm trees—but it took a while. In 1873, when the Atlantic Coastline Railroad came to this community, the first name given to it was

Toisnot, an Indian word meaning "tarry not."

Earlier, a community called Joyner's Depot had been a mile north. There were two property owners there who refused to sell land for a town, so would-be settlers moved to another site which had been obtained by Judge George Howard of Tarboro. Town residents planted elm trees all over the place, especially along the streets, and by 1891, Elm City had become the town's name.

In 1895, for some unknown reason, the depot went back to being called Toisnot. The final change came in 1913 when both post office and depot officials accepted Elm City.

After a change or two, Rowan County's China Grove took that name when it established the first post office in 1823. The name came from many chinaberry trees growing here. In 1846, they changed the name to Luthersville, but in 1849, folks brought back China Grove. Had a shorter, crisper sound to it, they said.

Ahhhh, the town name of Chinquapin in Duplin County can bring childhood memories for older residents all over the state. The chinquapin is a small nut about the size of a marble. It has a slick shiny black husk covered by a prickly burr until late summer or early fall, when the burr opens and the nut falls out.

The good news is that the nut's husk is so thin it can be cracked with the teeth and the kernel easily removed. The bad news is that the great blight long ago which destroyed so many of our American chestnut trees, also took many chinquapins. Chinquapin is the Algonquin Indian word for edible nut.

Union Grove Ridge in Iredell County was a campsite liked by the Indians. The Blue Ridge Mountains, Brushy Mountains, and the pinnacle of Pilot Mountain are all visible from here. Pilot Mountain is about sixty miles away from the small town of Union Grove that grew on the ridge. An earlier name was Indian Hill.

Union Grove may have once been called Blackjack, but not for the oak tree of that name. Rather, for the blackjack leather whip used to keep order. There was a well in the forks of the road and a trading post nearby at that time, and travelers between Wilkesboro and Salisbury stopped there. Sometimes they quarrelled and fought and authorities wielded the blackjack whip.

One accounting for the Union Grove name is that Union sympathizers lived here.

And still another is that slaves of the area, newly emancipated, gathered to worship by an outdoor union arbor they built by a grove of fir trees. "Let's go down to the Union Grove," they would say to each other.

There is a Black Jack in Pitt County that got its name sometime around 1831. Several local men were building a church and while they worked they talked about choosing a community name. Blackjack oaks grew all around the church. When a workman on the church roof threw his hatchet and it stuck in one of the trees, someone asked, "Why not call this place Blackjack?"

Early on in Madison County, the community of Walnut was known as Jewel Hill. Not because of precious gemstones, although the area is likely rich in those if you know where to look.

Actually, the name started as Duel Hill because that's where two cattle drovers fought a duel. Somehow, "duel" wound up mispronounced as "jewel." When a post office came to Jewel Hill, residents had to change the name. "There's already a Jewel Hill post office," said the bureaucrats in charge of approving place names. "You'll need to pick something else."

Folks looked around and saw all their fine walnut trees,

and not too far away they saw the Walnut Mountains named for the trees, so Walnut seemed a good choice.

22
Critters, Wild and Domestic

Wildcats once roamed our state, and some of these big cats remain in remote regions. Old-timers tell of hearing wildcats call in the night—like a woman's scream, they describe the sound, enough to make your hair stand on end.

Perhaps the big cats followed the rough trail from one mountain to another in Macon County, which is why we continue to call the trail The Catstairs.

We commemorate the wildcat with Cat Pen Gap and Cat Ridge in Transylvania County, and Cat Pen Branch in Madison County. In Macon County, Cat Creek rises and flows into Rabbit Creek.

Cat Square, a country crossroads in early Lincoln County, was not named for the wildcat, but for a litter of hapless kittens abandoned there.

A brave dog inspired the names of Hanging Dog Creek, Hanging Dog Mountain, Hanging Dog Gap and Hanging Dog Community in Cherokee County. This is the story Cherokee Indians tell of a hunter and his faithful dog:

Long ago a terrible winter brought famine and the threat of starvation to the Cherokee people. Their corn crop had failed, leaving game as the major food source. But the hunters, too, had problems. Game was scarce and they were unable to bring home enough food for the village.

One hunter by the name of Deer Killer was more successful than the others and frequently brought meat to his cabin. His success had more to do with his dog than with his prowess as a hunter. The dog would never give up. It would fight a bear and hold it at bay until its master came. It would chase a deer through the gap where Deer Killer waited, or scratch out a fat groundhog for the pair to take home.

But there came a day, late in the winter of this dreadful time, when Deer Killer and his dog went on their daily hunt and searched for many miles before finally coming upon a deer. The dog chased it but couldn't get it to run in the right direction.

The dog tried again and again but the big buck could not be steered through the gap where Deer Killer waited with his bow. A heavy rain began and already swollen streams began to rise. Finally, at dusk, the deer ran through the gap and Deer Killer shot it, but the arrow did not pierce its heart.

The badly wounded buck ran towards a nearby creek with the little dog close behind. Deer Killer followed and arrived in time to see the deer crawling out of the creek on the other side.

But Deer Killer's dog was no longer on its heels. The dog was trapped in a mass of jammed logs, drift vines and debris in the middle of the stream, unable to swim and in danger of drowning.

Deer Killer plunged into the stream, struggling against the icy rushing waters to free the dog. Together they swam across the stream and took up the trail of the wounded buck.

Many cold, weary hours later, they found the buck. That night Deer Killer shared fresh meat with the starving camp. There was much rejoicing—and the villagers decided to name all the nearby landmarks for the hanging dog that had saved them.

While Flat Rock community in Vance County wasn't

named for a canine, John Bullock Watkins, Jr., tells a story about how his grandfather's dog helped to provide the name.

At one time the main road through the area crossed a big flat rock. The dog could recognize the sound of his owner's buggy wheels crossing that rock, and as soon as he heard it he gave a welcoming yelp.

That became the signal to Watkins' cook to put the bread in the oven and she always had his supper ready when he walked in.

Some say that a community called Rabbit Shuffle exists in Caswell County. It's called that, they tell you while grinning from ear to ear, because the place is so poor a rabbit has to shuffle to stay alive. More than likely, these are the same folk who tell you about Hardscrabble, which they say is a place in Yancey County where the rocky soil is so hard to till that early settlers had a "hard scrabble" making a living.

Grey squirrels abound in Avery County. So many romped along one swift, winding creek that settlers named it after the bushy-tailed rodents. A Squirrel Creek also runs in Lenoir County, and Squirrel Branches flow in Gaston, Guilford, and Madison Counties.

Might as well mention Squirrel Gap in Transylvania County and Squirrels (yes, plural) Gap in Madison.

Boomer is the nickname of a little red mountain squirrel, kissing cousin, no doubt, to the grey squirrel. Wilkes County postmaster Boomer Matheson got his nickname from the squirrel's. And the town of Boomer, once known as Warrior Creek, was named for him.

Why, oh why, would a place be named Frog Level?

Such a place exists in Pitt County. The answer to the question, according to Charles Edwards in *The State* magazine, March, 1979, is this:

"Because it's a suitable place for frogs and fine people."
Another explanation holds that it was because this was a flat, swampy place.

Would that apply to spots in areas far more hilly than Pitt County that also were once called Frog Level? That was the case for Oakland in Rutherford County, as well as for Clingman in Wilkes County, which was officially named for Congressman Thomas L. Clingman.

Ask how Cashiers in mountainous Jackson County got its name and you'll likely hear about a horse, a mule, or some bull—well, one particular bull.

One story tells of a famous racehorse named Cash who was put out to pasture in a lush valley there after his glory days were over. Folks started calling the spot "Cash's Valley," which eventually got shortened to Cashiers.

Another version argues that it wasn't a horse, but a dependable mule named Cash from whom the town got its name. Yet another claims that it was a popular bull named Casius who provided the name after dying of a broken neck when his horns became entangled in vines.

If none of the above suits, what about this? The town was named for a man named Cashiers (a hermit, some say) who once lived there.

The name of Buzzard Town in McDowell County is easily explained. A farmer who lived there long ago lost his cattle to accidental poisoning. In those days dead animals were not buried, just left to let nature take its course. Nature's course was buzzards—so many of them that people in the area never forgot the sight. The place has been called Buzzard Town ever since.

In another part of McDowell County is the Goose Creek Community, also named in the early days. Settlers along this creek kept a generous supply of geese, using them for food, and plucking their down and feathers for bedding.

Picture a place where bears get together to socialize and take it easy. An early settler by the name of William Mills came across such a spot in Henderson County. He returned to watch the bears roll playfully in the dirt and scratch themselves. Mills named several places during his North Carolina travels. He called this one Bear Wallow, and it's still called that.

During the Revolution, British General Charles Cornwallis raided the plantation of J. J. Edmondson in Greene County. Edmondson turned his prize bull loose on the troops, hoping to scare them off.

The bull was no match for the soldiers, who killed it and hung the head in a treetop where it stayed for several years.

Edmondson survived, though, and wryly began calling his home Bulls Head. The area adopted the name and eventually became Bulls Head Township.

In Avery County, Cow Camp was where early settlers fed their cattle in spring before the grass came in. When there was a shortage of hay and fodder, cattle owners cut down linden trees and fed the cattle the roughage.

Buffalo Ford is a rural community in the Coleridge Township of southeastern Randolph County. Local tradition is that this was where first the buffalo, then Indians, and finally white settlers crossed Deep River. Buffalo Ford became known as the best crossing between Franklinville and the Moore County line.

Most buffalo were gone by 1750, when settlers first came to this area. Some say the last buffalo killed here was at Reuben Cox farm, which was later owned by Tom Hodgin.

• • •

The last elk in North Carolina is believed to have been killed in 1781 by William Davenport of Caldwell County. Davenport was only twelve years old at the time but already an expert marksman and hunter. There must have been large numbers of elk in the state at one time for "elk" is used in many place names. A few are Elk River, Elk Creek, Elk Mountain, Elk Park, Elk Shoals, Elkville, and yes, Elk Wallow.

In colonial times, an area of Richmond County became overrun with wolves. What to do? Several farmers got together and constructed a trapping pit. Perhaps they should have put up a "For Wolves Only" sign. Wily wolves eluded the pit, but it snared a farmer's mule. (It's doubtful that the mule could read, anyway.) The unsuccessful trap didn't last long, but mention of it did. The area eventually became known as Wolf Pit Township.

Duck in Dare County near Currituck Sound got its name for the wild ducks in the area.

Swan Quarter, county seat of Hyde County, may have been named for the swans once found around Swan Quarter Bay. Some, however, claim the place was named for Samuel F. Swann, a landowner in the area.

Swancreek, in Yadkin County, was named by residents who mistook the many wild geese on nearby streams as swans.

Mitchell County's Wing owes no credit to fowl or other feathered creatures. The name honors Charles Hallet Wing (1836-1915) who settled in the area and opened the first free public library (about 15,000 volumes) in the state.

23
Flowers and Other Flora

Sweet wild violets growing in Currituck County were the inspiration for the name of the Outer Banks town called Corolla. In 1895, the Postal Department requested three name suggestions for the community's new post office.

One submission was Jones Hill, in honor of a local citizen. Another was Currituck Beach. The third was for the showy, colorful petals (called the corolla) of the area's wild violet. Somebody at the Postal Department must have had an eye for beauty, for that was the suggestion accepted.

Another community in Currituck County also was named for flowers—the abundant waterlilies in ditches and ponds. It's called Waterlily.

A Cherokee County community also chose to honor violets with its name: Violet.

Pink Hill in Lenoir County isn't where it used to be. The original Pink Hill developed around the residence of a man named Anthony Davis who lived on a hill where pink wildflowers bloomed each spring, prompting people who lived nearby to call their community Pink Hill.

After the railroad came through, though, most residents of the community moved a couple of miles down the tracks to a new location. They took the name with them. Nobody remembers what the pink wildflower was called.

Martin County's Beargrass is named for a type of yucca plant (Bear Grass) that grows here. The county's Bear Grass Swamp was a part of the large tract of land received by one of the first settlers, John Swinson, from the Earl of Granville in 1761.

The first name of Calabash, the famous seafood restaurant town in Brunswick County, was Pea Landing. Settlers came here before 1880, and they took the name not from peas but from the peanuts shipped from the town's docks to Wilmington.

Nobody knows for sure why townspeople changed the name to Calabash early in the 1900s. It may have been because of the wild gourds by that Indian name that grew in the area. These gourds were dried and cut into dippers for drinking the cool water drawn from local wells. It also may have been because the town's location in the crook of the river was similar to the shape of the gourd.

The "poison" of Ashe County's Poison Branch didn't affect humans. The branch got the name because of the wild parsnips growing along its banks that were poisonous to cattle.

Maiden, in Catawba County, got its name from Maiden Creek, where the banks were covered with maiden-cane fern (*Poaceae hemitomon*).

24
Springs

"Eupeptic Springs water is an alternative medicine, gradually inducing a change in the constitution and restoring the healthy functions of the stomach and bowels without noticeable evacuations." Wow.

By the time those words appeared in an advertising brochure for Iredell County's Eupeptic Springs, the place had become a thriving health resort and the water had won a silver medal for excellence at the 1904 St. Louis Exposition.

The Catawba Indians called the waters Powder Springs because they said the brackish taste was like gunpowder. (They tasted gunpowder?) Dr. John F. Foard, one time owner of the springs, changed the name to the Greek word "Eupeptic," meaning "good digestion."

Eupeptic Springs still flow gently in northern Iredell County, west of Olin. They are covered by tangled underbrush and go untasted except by wildlife. On the wooded hillside above are a few stone foundation remains of cabins used during the health resort era.

The Indians called another set of Iredell County springs Poison Springs because they noticed that deer and other wildlife wouldn't drink from them. In 1887, Donald McRae of Wilmington bought the springs and the 100-room hotel built earlier by entrepreneur R. L. Goodman. McRae changed the Poison name to the more aesthetic Barium Springs.

In 1883, a local newspaper wrote about Barium Springs: "It is doubted if so many different kinds of water are found within the same area anywhere else. There are barium, red, white and blue sulphur, chalybeate, alum, iron, limestone and freestone—eight springs with eight varieties of water, none of them ten steps from the other."

The hotel burned to the ground in November 1891. By World War I, the days of Barium Springs as a health resort and spa were over.

The waters of seven springs in Halifax County were named Aurelian meaning "golden" for their alleged cure-all properties, and the nearby community became known as Aurelian.

The clear, sparkling waters of Silver Springs in Gates County inspired the name for springs and community. The bubbling waters of a cluster of springs in Cleveland County led to the Cherokee calling them Boiling Springs. The town that surrounds them bears that name. The town of Chalybeate Springs in Harnett County was named for nearby springs containing chalybeate, salts of iron.

Connelly Springs in Burke County was known as Happy Home before its development as a health resort using the springs' mineral waters. The Connelly family developed the resort and named it after Mrs. William L. Connelly. Eagle Springs in Moore County got its name from the Eagle family who lived near the mineral springs. Holly Springs, a town in Wake County, was named for holly trees growing near a spring. There are also communities called Holly Springs in Carteret, Henderson, Rutherford, and Yadkin counties.

First called Warm Springs for its thermal springs, this Madison County town became a health resort around 1800. A rise in area economics turned up water temperature, too. Before long, the name was changed to Hot Springs.

Alleghany County's town of Laurel Springs got its name from area springs and laurel thickets. Wake County's Willow Spring was named in the 1800s for the many willow trees nearby.

Mill Spring, originally spelled with an "s" on Mill, is a town in Polk County and named for the son of pioneer William Mills. Bottled water from Stokes County's Moores Creek was once in demand for its alleged health-promoting properties. The Moore family owned the springs and the town of Moores Creek was named for the springs. Patterson Springs, a town in Cleveland County, was named for early resident Arthur Patterson, Sr.

Before Mount Vernon Springs in Chatham County was named for the home of George Washington it was called Hickory Springs and Ore Hill.

Once known as Fair Grounds, the Richmond County town of Ellerbe Springs was named after W. T. Ellerbe, a South Carolinian, who built a summer health resort there in the 1800s. The attraction was the natural spring water, long touted by locals as curing hay fever and various ailments. When the railroad came through around 1911, Ellerbe became the station and community name. The springs are still active.

Mineral Springs Community in Greene County and the town of Mineral Springs in Union County were named for springs containing...well, rule out animal and vegetable.

The first name of this town in Wayne County was Whitehall. William Whitfield was responsible for that. He settled here in 1743, built a big house and painted it gloriously white. Later Jim Parker, while deer hunting in 1815, came across several leisurely-flowing springs—seven of them. Each spring had a different mineral content and people who drank from the springs attributed miraculous cures for ailments. By

1880, people were coming to the springs and using the place as a health resort.

Eventually a 100-room resort hotel was built near the seven springs and stayed in operation until 1944. The town was called Seven Springs long before the name became official in 1951.

Eli Barker knew he was thirstier than usual one July day in 1885. After all, plowing a steep hillside in Ashe County in the summer time can work up a sweat. Even so, Barker was pleasantly surprised at the taste of the water his son Willie brought him. Eli turned up the tin cup and drank every drop. "Could you get me some more, son?" Eli asked.

It tickled Willie that his Pa liked the water. Willie had walked a long ways down this little branch to find a spring, so he could take his Pa a good, cold cupful. He'd found the spring when he saw water running down a rock. Willie's arms and hands were hurting from poison ivy sores, but no matter. He scratched out a hole beneath the rock and filled the cup with water. The water that splashed on the sores felt soothing.

The next morning Willie's sores were healed. Soon word of this spread beyond the community of Crumpler where the Barkers lived, and people began coming in search of the medicinal waters, some bringing ailing livestock. Out-of-state newspapers wrote about the spring, causing more people to come.

Finally, Captain C. V. Thompson from Virginia bought this spring and others nearby and enclosed them. He had the water analyzed and disclosed his findings.

The water contained bromine, arsenic, lithia, iodine, potash, and a phosphate. "It is a dead shot to indigestion and all stomach and kidney troubles, or diseases from impure blood," he claimed.

Over the years, the medicinal powers of the springs became widely known and the property changed hands many times. Nearby springs were called All Healing Springs. Healing Springs Hotel, built in 1888, became a popular resort. The hotel burned in 1962. Today, the mineral springs water is still available.

This was not the only place in the state to be called All Healing Springs and Healing Springs. Another Healing Springs community is in Davidson County. All Healing Springs community in Alexander County was a popular health resort in the late nineteenth and early twentieth centuries, as was All Healing Springs community in Gaston County.

Now the truth about Maggot Spring. Sure, there were larvae of some insect in the spring water that long-, long-ago-day when cattle rangers happened onto the spring in what is now Great Smoky Mountains National Park.

But that didn't mean a positive I. D. of maggots. One little negative rumor and the first thing you know you've got Maggot Spring, Maggot Spring Gap, and Maggot Ridge.

Part IV

Historical, Fictional, and Just Because

25
Creeks

Nash County's Pigbasket Creek isn't newly named. Anything but that, since "Pigbasket" appears in deeds dating before 1760. This is one story about the name:

An early settler owned a sow that gave birth to a litter in a patch of woods. After he found them, he wanted to move them to shelter. But how? You don't move a hefty sow and brood easily, especially if you have to cross a swollen stream by footlog to get home.

"Aha," perhaps the settler told himself, "I'll gather the piglets in a big basket, and Mama Pig will follow me home." So he put the piglets in a basket, called to Mama Pig and off they went. All seemed well until he got to the footlog across the creek.

When the settler started across the log, the sow grew concerned for her brood and charged. Sow, settler and the basket of piglets ended up in the creek. Fortunately, Mama and all her babies were saved; the settler, too, and the creek evermore had a name.

A creek in eastern Rutherford County puzzled early settlers. It had patches of quicksand all along its path, and the settlers wondered whether they and their horses could cross it safely. It took a long time to find all the quicksand pits and map them so the fording spots could be marked. Such a hassle was it that they forever called the stream Puzzle Creek.

• • •

The waters of Slow Creek in Cherokee County actually are lively and sparkling as they flow near Braden Mountain. But this was such a tranquil place to live, say the people of Slow Creek community, so far off the fast track, that a name like Speedy Creek would never do.

An errant tropical storm once blew through Clay County felling all the trees along a particular stream, which is why it's now called Hurricane Creek.

People in Avery County say that Three Mile Creek actually is that long.

Calico Creek in Carteret County got its name courtesy of a shipwreck. Long ago, an English vessel wrecked near Beaufort and storm tides washed the cargo ashore. When the storm passed, residents anxiously rushed outside to determine damages and found the ship's cargo of cloth draped like festive banners over bushes along a creek. It was the first calico that many of the residents had seen.

The name of Sleepy Creek in Wayne County doesn't describe the way the waters flow. One story is that Indians thought the springs feeding this creek had medicinal qualities. Sick persons would come to the creek, drink the waters, and lie down on the banks to sleep and recuperate.

Another version is that nearby still operators used the creek water to make their product. And wow! Was it good! So good, that customers couldn't wait to get home with their purchases. They'd imbibe on the spot and stretch out by the creek to sleep it off.

Stinking Quarters Creek in Alamance County may have been named for a Mr. Stankins or Stauken who owned a quarter of the land in this vicinity. Then there's the other story. The one about Indian hunters who used to butcher game here. They left the unwanted carcass parts to the elements and to, well, you know, *stink*.

More than likely Swearing Creek in Davidson County got its name because a family named Swearingen settled on the creek headwaters—and the original name was Swearingen Creek.

The other story is that traders crossing the creek here to go into Indian territory swore that they wouldn't tattle on each other's rowdy behavior while they were away from home.

Family names frequently have been used for streams. Blevins Creek, Hensons Creek, Wilsons Creek, Anthonys Creek, and Gouges Creek, for example, are in Avery County and named for families who once lived near them.

McDowell County's Chalk Creek is called that because of the soft white rock found along its banks. From the days of its discovery, settlers used the chalk-like rock to mark home-spun for sewing or to rub on anything that needed a temporary mark.

Snow Creek community in Iredell County got its name from historic Snow Creek Church, and the church got its name from the creek that runs through the area. The water in the creek is "pure as snow," some say, while others say the name is because snow melts slowly along the creek's shady banks.

Another Snow Creek in Mitchell County flows into the North Toe River, but it got its name from snow white rocks that lie along its bed.

And what about Lodawick Oakes and his wife, Dora, who once lived near a creek in Avery County? Busy folks were they, burning willow switches and making gun powder. They accumulated so much money from their venture that they bought themselves a slave. The creek is still called Powder Mill.

In Pasquotank County, New Begun Creek may have been named for Newbeggin, a town in Yorkshire, England, where some original settlers were from. Or a Quaker named Boyd may have had something to do with the name. It is told that Boyd had a quarrel with his neighbors and moved himself lock, stock, and barrel, to the banks of the creek to make a fresh start. Boyd's "new beginning" may be the name of the creek shortened with use to New Begun.

No doubt, there are more Madison County Creeks than one with steep sides but the incline of this creek contributed to its name. Long ago, there was a Madison County boy who dearly loved horses. He was a little on the wild side, though, and his father complained constantly about the boy's recklessness—particularly when it came to showing off on horseback.

Now, the boy really wanted to please his father, so he thought up different ways to show that he could be as responsible as the next person. "Let me take the corn to the mill this time, Pa," he begged one day. "I'll ride old Buster steady as you please and be back before you know it." So, his father agreed and they put the bags of corn across old Buster's rump and off the boy went to the mill.

Well, he had to cross this steep-sided creek to get to the mill and try as he mightily did, he couldn't keep corn from spilling off the horse's back. He struggled and worked and got off Buster, trying to catch corn as it fell from the bags and sailed off down the creek. Despite his efforts, he got wet and lost a lot of corn. Nevertheless, he went on to the mill and had the remainder of the corn ground. He returned home with pitifully few sacks of milled corn.

Pa was mad, but the boy had an excuse. "It was all the fault of that old Spill Corn Creek, Pa," he argued.

26
Mistakes Happen

Across the street from Bearwallow Baptist Church in Henderson County is the location of the first post office in the community of Gerton—except this post office was called Pump, not Gerton.

It was Pump for nineteen years, named for an actual working pump—an important pump, because it supplied water off the mountain to the whole valley. Who knows but that the place would still be known as Pump, if not for some fancy handwriting?

In 1902, postmaster George S. Wall requested a canceling stamp for the office, a postmark. He was an accomplished calligrapher of the old school, which called for a flowing style of writing with the more flourishes and curlicues the better.

He almost outdid himself filling out the requisition form. A squiggle here, a long tail and twist there—oh, the form was a masterpiece of artistic writing.

The postmaster could scarcely wait for his new postmark to arrive. When it did, he began to stamp with a joyous fervor. Whomp, whomp, whomp. The sound of the stamp against paper was music to his ears. Then he froze. His gorgeous new stamp was displaying the wrong message.

"Rump, North Carolina," it printed. "Rump, Rump, Rump."

Shortly after word got around about the new stamp

that embarrassingly misnamed the community, and everybody'd had a good laugh about it, talk started about renaming the community. Folks said they'd honored their pump long enough. After all, it didn't even know it was being honored. Maybe they ought to call the place after a real live person, somebody who made a contribution.

Why not Gertrude, for Miss Gertrude Freeman, long-time resident and well-liked teacher?

Miss Freeman's brother said there was a problem with calling the place by his sister's first name, though. She was extremely modest and likely would be embarrassed to have her name so commonly used. "I suggest we combine her name with the word 'town' and call it Gerton," he said.

Fancy handwriting also resulted in the name of Corapeake for a community in Gates County. Its earlier names were Pleasant Hill, Orapeake (for a local Indian tribe) and Jonesville.

When the post office came to the community, the residents decided to go back to the Orapeake name. The postmaster filled out the paperwork with fine calligraphy and sent the request to postal officials.

The postmark came back Corapeake, and rather than endure the trouble of trying to change it, the community decided to accept it.

No telling what happened back in 1899 when Arch Eudy applied for a post office in his Stanly County community. He put down on the request form, plain as you please, that he wanted the place named Eudy.

So, what did he get? Endy. And Endy Community it is to this day.

Could have been a need for bifocals when somebody at the Post Office Department dropped an "e" from this Cleveland County post office name request.

Residents knew what they wanted. They wanted their community named for Julius Caesar. "Caesar" sounded dignified, historical, and besides, the word rolled nicely off the tongue.

But the postmark came with a missing "e": Casar. In 1973, a new charter finally made Casar the official name. After all, folks had been calling it that for many years.

Aaron MacDuff was an early settler to Haywood County. He came from Scotland and was an all-round good man. Folks admired his hunting skills and the way he fell right in and gave a helping hand to neighbors. Smart, too, the way he read a lot but didn't brag about it—just gave book-learning advice if somebody asked for it. And folks loved the way he could entertain for hours with his tall tales.

The area where he settled became known as Aaron Duff's Bend and that's the name it went by for years. When in 1873 the place needed an official name for the new post office, residents wanted to keep the name but it was too long. "Let's drop the 'Bend' but keep Aaron Duff," somebody suggested, and all agreed. They sent the application to Washington and thought the matter settled.

They got a surprise, though, when they learned the name that had been approved: Iron Duff.

Semora is in Caswell County, named in 1877 for postmaster James Morrison McAden's young daughter.

An unusual name, Semora. Her descendants tell this story:

When she was born in 1871, relatives in Texas sent congratulations. They had picked up a little Spanish in Texas and suggested naming the baby "Senora," most likely with tongue in cheek.

Maybe the suggested name in the letter appeared to be

Semora, or the parents simply put a creative twist on "senora," but that's how a North Carolina community got that name.

While Mashoes in Dare County may have inherited its name from an Indian village listed on John White's map in 1585 as "Mashawatoc," it could have been named for Peter Michieux and his family who were shipwrecked near here in 1739.

With his wife and child clinging to him, Michieux washed ashore and lost consciousness on the beach. When he came to, he found his family lying dead nearby. Michieux moved to the mainland and lived there for twenty years, but he never recovered from the trauma of losing his family.

At the end of his life he was a recluse and died sitting beneath a cypress tree. His skeleton, with his back against the tree, was discovered several years after his death. Nearby was a board with the story of his wife's and daughter's deaths carved into it. Could Mashoes be a mispronunciation of Michieux?

It could be that the Poga area of Avery County, including Poga (or Pogey) Mountain, got the name from a man who had been lost on the mountain for days and returned home ticked off about having taken the scenic route.

"I've been to pogey," he complained. In English dialect, pogey means boggy or sloppy.

Or the area could have been named for a fellow whose last name was Poga, according to another story. North Carolinians thought they were naming the place for one of their own. Turned out differently. When all the facts were known, it was learned that Mr. Poga lived in East Tennessee.

27
Change Happens

Flea Hill in Cumberland County got that name for good reason, people said. At the local tavern, the central gathering place, the owner allowed goats and hogs to freely roam the premises. Fleas on the animals infested humans, as well.

Later, times and the flea situation changed, and so did the name, to Eastover Township.

Early settlers of a Gates County town were known as rough-and-ready folks who, if they felt an itch, scratched. They had a sense of humor, too, and when a citizen said he was from "Scratch Hall," they laughed and said they were, too.

Of course, Scratch Hall is not a name you'd want to live with forever, so when townsfolk got ready for a permanent name, they called the place Eure.

A lot of settlements started out being called The Crossroads, which happened to one community in Surry County. Finally, residents decided they needed a more identifiable name, but what?

Professor E. P. McLeod, principal of Franklin School was one of those pushing for a new name in 1927. To him, calling the place "Crossroads" was like calling a boy, "boy," or a girl, "girl."

One evening while shopping at Hutchens Store, Professor McLeod picked up a loaf of bread for breakfast and came up with what he thought would be a perfect name.

"Let's call the place Toast," he said, and they did.

In the early 1900s, Few Community in Durham County had a railroad station and the Japanese city name of Oyama. After the December 7th, 1941, attack on Pearl Harbor by the Japanese, residents immediately changed the name to honor Dr. William P. Few, first president of Duke University.

There certainly was talk during World War II by the residents of the tiny settlement of Japan (along Wolf and Panther Creeks close to the Swain County line in Graham County) about changing the name of their post office.

They were annoyed that outsiders came to the post office to mail large quantities of letters bearing the postmark Japan.

Many wanted to change the name to McArthur in honor of World War II hero General Douglas McArthur. The name change never took place because plans were set in motion for building Fontana Dam and the village ended up covered by water.

Our Japan, incidentally, probably got its name from a variety of wild clover that flourished around the community. It wasn't good for hay or grazing and only grew in certain places. The clover's name was "Jaypan" (Lespedeza striata).

Burrtown may have had the first post office in Cleveland County. It was a settlement on the Broad River near Quinn's (later Ellis') Ferry named for Aaron Burr, who disgraced himself in 1804 when he shot Alexander Hamilton in a duel. When Burrtown grew into a town, residents changed the name to Erwinville, apparently in honor of local residents. Later, the town was renamed Dellinger for postmaster John P. Dellinger.

• • •

Sometimes place names had to be changed to avoid confusion with other places. Such was the case with Jerome in Johnston County. This settlement began around 1890 and got its name from Jerome Creech who owned land there. But another place in Bladen County also was named Jerome, so the Johnston County folks renamed their small place Micro.

Siler City, in Chatham County, was named for local landowner Samuel Siler, but it had several earlier names. It was first called Matthews Crossroads, for Captain Billy Matthews who lived at the intersection where the Raleigh-Salisbury and Greensboro-Fayetteville stage roads crossed. It was later called Siler's Store and after the railway came, the settlement became known as Siler Station. The first post office bore that name but was frequently confused with another post office, Silver Station.

In 1884, residents changed the town's name to Siler City. In those days, Siler City was the rabbit shipping center of the State, but that never entered the debate about choosing a new name for the town, which nowadays ships processed chickens instead of rabbits.

Goose Nest was the original name of Oak City in Martin County. Or so goes the legend.

During the Civil War, Union soldiers marching from a nearby raid stopped at a crossroads and set up camp in an abandoned building. There they discovered a goose on its nest. They moved their camp so as not to disturb the goose.

In 1892 Goose Nest incorporated as Conoho, an Indian name from nearby Conoho Creek. The town became Oak City in 1905 because of mail delivery confusion between Conoho and Conetoe in Edgecombe County.

Townspeople supposedly chose "Oak City" because someone noticed the name on a calendar advertising Oak City Laundry in Raleigh. Another story is that Oak City is named for the many beautiful oak trees lining the streets.

Robeson County's Maxton must hold some record for name changes. In the town's first twenty-five years, it was known as Shoe Heel Depot (1862), Shoe Heel, Tilden, Quhele, Shoe Heel (again), then Mackstown, and finally, Maxton in 1887.
Shoe Heel came from nearby Shoe Heel Creek, supposedly named because the creek had many crooks shaped like a shoe heel. Tilden came from Samuel J. Tilden, a former Governor of New York and a locally popular Democratic nominee for president in 1876.
The origin of Quhele is unknown but perhaps was the Scottish pronunciation of "Shoe Heel."
By 1887 the place was known as Mackstown because of the many residents who had the Scottish prefix "Mac" or "Mc" to their names. Postal authorities made the name official with Maxton.

The town of Bunnlevel in Harnett County was named ironically for a man who lived on a hill. Bunn's first name is unknown, but he once lived on Dollar's Hill (his daughter married a man named Dollar) about a mile north of the settlement that later was named for him. Bunn was involved in bringing the railroad to the area, and he moved his family to level land near the spot where the new station was being built. Some people wanted to call the town Spur, because that was what the railroad line was, but people started calling it Bunn's Level and that stuck. The name became Bunnlevel when the town was incorporated in 1921.

28
Storms, Shipwrecks, and Natural Events

During the Civil War, the *Maple Leaf*, a Federal transport ship carrying 101 Confederate prisoners ran aground on Currituck Beach. More than half of the prisoners escaped and made their way inland.

Local people quickly came to the aid of the escapees and led them to hideouts in nearby swamps. Before long though, Federal soldiers in search of their prisoners were camping on the Currituck Courthouse lawn. Some escapees died resisting capture. Others died from illness and were buried in concealed graves by local people.

Federal soldiers burned portions of courthouse records and stole others, taking them north. In 1950, Currituck County recovered some of these records, paying $25 for their return. In 1976, Ohio returned some old deeds.

The community that aided the Confederate soldiers was called Long House Corner. The "long house" was a directional landmark in the middle of the community and belonged to Sally White, who housed slaves there. Long House Corner remained the name until 1900 when the first post office became Maple in honor of the residents' efforts to save the soldiers from the *Maple Leaf*.

Another Maple community is in central Washington County.

•••

Some say the sinking of a Federal transport steamship in 1862 provided the name for Pamlico County's town of Oriental. The ship sank near Bodie Island and the transom of the ship washed up on the beach and was found by Rebecca Midgett, wife of the town's first settler, "Uncle Lou" Midgett.

Maybe it was Uncle Lou or Rebecca who nailed the nameplate to a tree in the intersection of the settlement. At any rate, people started using the nameplate for direction. "Go to the Oriental sign and take a right...." Oriental became the name selected for the village when the first post office opened.

When the three-masted schooner, *John S Woods*, foundered on the shoals off Currituck County in 1895, residents of a nearby beach settlement spent three days getting a lifeline to the ship in stormy weather. They managed to save all on board, but the vessel was doomed. It broke up and washed ashore.

Using lumber and materials from the ship, John Waterfield, a duck carver from Knotts Island, built a church and called it Wash Woods Church. The settlement became known as Wash Woods, too.

While one storm brought the community good fortune and a name, others brought about its end. Wind and high seas overwhelmed the settlement's fertile fields and woods with sand and salt, making it impossible for the residents to raise crops and livestock. They abandoned Wash Woods for other areas.

"If it be predestined that there be a wreck on the Atlantic Coast, please let it be here," a preacher named Starr supposedly prayed during the winter of 1813.

"Here" was the community of Straits in Carteret County, and Starr was a Methodist minister calling upon God to save its starving residents. A drought the previous summer had killed crops, and a severe winter had brought fishing to a halt. To further complicate matters, the Napoleonic Wars and a

British blockade prevented trade.

A few days after the minister's prayer, a ship carrying a cargo of flour wrecked nearby, saving the community.

Straits was named for the narrow strip of land between the mainland and Harkers Island.

In the 1800s, a ship carrying rice went aground on the east end of Bogue Banks in Carteret County. People scurried to the beach to salvage the cargo, creating a path from one side of the island to the other. The place became known as Rice Path. Storms later eroded the area, forcing residents to move to a wider expanse of land, and Rice Path disappeared. It stood in what is now the town of Emerald Isle.

Some of Rice Path's residents moved a couple of miles up the beach to a settlement that later became known as Salter Path.

Riley Salter, his wife Julia, and daughter, Annie, moved to this spot on the Bogue Banks in the 1880s. He built a small frame house near the sound and settled into a fisherman's life. Julia and the other women in the settlement split and gutted the fish their husbands caught and carried them to the ocean for washing.

The fish were salted and packed in wooden barrels. Then men carried them back to the sound to await a boat from Hyde County that brought sweet potatoes and corn in trade for the fish. The men carried the barrels on long poles that rested on their shoulders, and the path they took passed right by Riley Salter's house. People started calling the area Salter's Path, and Salter Path is the name of the resort town today.

Oregon Inlet in Dare County connects Pamlico Sound to the Atlantic Ocean at the southern tip of Bodie Island and the northern tip of Pea Island. It was opened by a hurricane in 1846, and for a time it remained nameless.

Then a merchant from Little Washington, W. H.

Willard, purchased a steamboat named the *Oregon* in New York and started home with it. As he approached the coast north of Hatteras, a major storm blew up. Could he pass safely through the new inlet in this storm? He felt he had no choice but to plunge ahead. His ship became the first to pass through the inlet and gave it its name.

29
Indian Stories

Several North Carolina counties carry the names of Native American tribes who once lived there. Among them are the counties of Alleghany, Cherokee, Catawba, Chowan, Currituck (perhaps), Pamlico, Pasquotank (perhaps), Perquimans, and Watauga. Each tribe left its mark on the whole of our heritage, but none left a richer trove of oral history and legend than the Cherokee. Here are four Cherokee stories of North Carolina place names:

Standing Indian Mountain rises 5,600 feet above sea level in Clay County and is called by many "the grandstand of the Southern Appalachians."

Once, a winged beast with glittering eyes and giant claws terrorized an Indian village. It spied a small group of children playing and swooped down, sinking his talons into the smallest child and snatched him, screaming, away.

People of the village were distraught. They kept their children close but even those efforts failed. The beast was too swift and unpredictable. He carried away more children to their deaths.

"We must do something," the people said. "We must find this beast and destroy him." So hunters tracked the beast to its den on the south slope of a mountain peak only to find it inaccessible.

The villagers stationed a brave to watch the den and returned to the village to pray for help. "Save us, Great Spirit," they asked. "Let our people no longer have to live with this dreadful fear."

A barrage of lightning bolts struck the mountaintop, setting it ablaze and killing the beast in his lair. So devastating was the fire that even today the peak remains bald.

The brave stationed there started to flee his post when the first bolts split the air. His punishment was severe and everlasting. He stands, in stone, at his vigil site keeping eternal watch.

Chief Kenocoonk's son, Wabajanick, a strong young man, worried his father with his frequent absences from his village.

The reason for his disappearances became apparent when he returned one day bringing with him the daughter of Chief Lanamouski of the Catawba tribe who had been forbidden to have anything to do with the Cherokees.

But Kenocoonk and his people accepted the young woman and gave a wedding feast for the couple near the top of tall cliffs overlooking a waterfall. In the midst of the celebration, angry Catawbas came to reclaim the bride.

The attack was short because the Cherokee were unarmed. But the bride and groom refused to be separated. They wrapped their arms around each other and jumped to their deaths from the cliffs.

Heartbroken and enraged, the Catawba chief ordered that the Cherokee prisoners be pushed off the cliffs as well. To assure no survivors, he had huge stones rolled off the cliffs to crush the bodies below.

The few Cherokee who escaped being captured later told of the horrifying screams of those pushed from the cliffs. They later took others to recover the bodies from the carnage site at the foot of the cliffs. They called the place "The Ball

Ground of the Evil Spirit."

The story passed down generation to generation. In more recent times, the sounds of the big stones crashing onto the bodies were likened to the noises of a bowling alley. That explains why this area in McDowell County is called Devil's Ball Alley.

The Cherokee called this mountain gap on the Haywood-Jackson County line *Ahalu'na* (place where they ambushed). It is now called Soco Gap. Likely, the gap was named after Haywood County's Soco Falls.

"Soco" is thought to be a corruption of the Cherokee word *sog-wah*, meaning "one," which is how many of De Soto's men the Cherokee threw over the falls.

The Cherokee used Soco Gap as a lookout and at one time ambushed a large party of invading Iroquois. They killed all the Iroquois except one, and as was the custom, the Cherokee cut off the survivor's ears and sent him home to tell his people what happened.

During the War of 1812, a tribal meeting instigated by the powerful Shawnee Indian Chief Tecumseh took place at Soco Gap. Tecumseh supported the British in the War and he, with some representatives of tribes north of the Ohio, traveled to the gap to enlist help from the Cherokees.

Tecumseh presented his case at a tribal council, but was overruled by Cherokee Chief Yonaguska who advised continued peace.

Tecumseh was so furious at the refusal that he sprang to his feet and left the council by jumping over the heads of the warriors seated around the chiefs.

Nan-toh-ee-yah-heh-lih means "Sun in the Middle" in Cherokee. The Nantahala Gorge in Graham and Swain Counties is so deep that the Indians believed that only the mid-day sun was strong enough to brighten its depths.

Uktena, a giant horned serpent who possessed a brilliant gem between its horns, lived there. The gem had qualities of good and evil and could cause death to the family of any person who simply looked upon it. But if the gem could be taken from the serpent's head, it would reveal the future to the person who possessed it.

One hunter dared to try to kill the serpent and claim the gem. He clothed himself in leather to protect his body and stealthily approached the serpent. Luckily, the serpent was asleep and the hunter leaped upon it, stabbing and fatally wounding it.

When the hunter tore the gem from the serpent's head, the serpent, in its death throes, twisted and rolled from one side of the gorge to the other. The force of the giant body against the sides of the canyon caused the shutting out of the sun and from that time on there has been only twilight in Nantahala Gorge.

30
Just Because

North Carolinians read more than the funny papers. Always have. So it's not surprising that books show up in our place names.

Will Shakespeare helped out with the name of Buncombe County's town of Arden. Not personally, you understand, but from the Forest of Arden in Shakespeare's play, "As You Like It." The community of Ivanhoe on the Black River in Sampson County got its name in the 1880s, courtesy of a reader of Sir Walter Scott's novel of the same name.

The name of the town of Calypso in Duplin County came from the sea nymph in Homer's *Odyssey*. Valhalla community in Polk County is for the mythological hall of Norse god Odin—the hall where souls of heroes slain in battle were received. A Valhalla community is also in Chowan County.

In Duplin County, a town once called Duplin Depot and then Mooresville became Warsaw after the Atlantic Coastline Railroad came through in the 1800s. This is what happened, according to say-so:

An early stationmaster was Thaddeus Love. His tenure came at the time Jane Porter's novel *Thaddeus of Warsaw* was popular, so someone suggested that since they already had Thaddeus, why not Warsaw?

You might not realize at first that the town of Watha in Pender County was originally Hiawatha. Residents can tell you about the historical Hiawatha, chief of the Onandaga Indians, who lived about 1575 and helped form the Iroquois Confederacy. Henry Wadsworth Longfellow made him the hero of his epic poem *The Song of Hiawatha*. Probably a reader of that poem proposed the name.

And why shouldn't we be well-read? Any state having places named Harvard, Yale, and Princeton could scarcely be less. Harvard Community is in Yancey County, Yale in Henderson County. We have two towns named Princeton— one in Johnston County and the other in Northampton. Were they named for those prestigious schools? Maybe.

Some people are so creative that all it takes for them to coin a word that becomes a lasting place name is to be asked. That's what happened when George Leidy Wood, executive vice-president of the Montvale Lumber Company back in 1902, turned to his wife and asked her to name the pretty little company tent-town set up alongside the Little Tennessee River on the Swain County side of a wilderness. Although the Woods had a home in Asheville, Mrs. Wood spent time with her husband in this location she loved.

The couple name-searched in rail and postal guides but every name they found was too ordinary for this beautiful spot. That's when Wood suggested that his wife coin a word.

Mrs. Wood later said, "I thought of the lovely, flowering glens, the waterfalls that looked like fountains, leaping from ledge to ledge and eventually worked out the word *Fontana*, a short word, musical, easy to spell."

The Fontana Village name has survived four previous lives, including being covered by the waters of man-made Fontana Lake and a move to another site, now in Graham County.

"Dugga-Lu" was what a Catawba County textile cotton mill called the coins it distributed for use in the company store in 1898. Dugga-lu would have been a wonderful name for the mill village. Instead, it ended up being called Brookford, a name derived by combining the last names of the two mill owners, Henry J. Holbrook and E. L. Shuford.

Several other places also got their names from combining parts of others: Rhodhiss, a town of two counties, Burke and Caldwell, was named for John Rhodes and George Hiss, who in the late 1800s built a cotton mill there. In Caldwell County, Treeland had its name changed to Whitnel honoring two local mill owners, J. O. White and J. L. Nelson. Town founders J. A. Macrae and A. A. Williford provided the name for the town of Raeford in Hoke County.

When a Gates County community needed a name, residents combined syllables from the Roberts Drug Company. In Richmond County, the town of Roberdel, is named for textile manufacturer, Robert L. Steele.

Doesn't it seem logical to name a town on the Virginia-Carolina border, Virgilina? Of course, and that is the name of this town in Granville County.

Who wouldn't agree that the Durham County town of Bahama needed a permanent name after being called Hunkadora, Balltown and Round Hill? That happened in the early twentieth century and came from combining syllables from names of three local families—Ball, Harris, and Mangum.

In Buncombe County, the town of Enka got its name from American Enka Corporation, who got its name by extracting the letters *N* and *K* from the company's official name, Nederlandsche Kunstzyde Fabricken.

While Hub may have been the center of activity long ago in Columbus County, that didn't account for the name. Hub came from the initials of H. U. Butters, who owned a large lumber plant there. The community later was renamed Boardman in honor of clergyman George Dana Boardman.

•••

You might call it a brotherly thing with the town names of Banner Elk, Hudson, Duncan, and Wadeville.

Take Avery County's Banner Elk. This place couldn't seem to decide on a name. The Indians called it Shawneehaw, and early settlers called it Upper Elk, Hix Improvement, Moses Deadening, and Larkin Chopping. This succession of names changed with the influx of Banners.

Martin Banner left the Piedmont to settle in this area along the Elk River just before the California gold discovery of 1849. He quickly came to love the area and sent back glowing letters to his five brothers encouraging them to join him. Within ten years all five brothers and their families had moved to the Elk River. With so many Banners around people started calling the place Banners Elk. Over time it became simply Banner Elk.

Lewis M. Banner is said to have owned seventeen slaves who were freed by Lincoln's Emancipation Proclamation. Another Banner relative was Dr. M. R. Banner who moved from Dalton, Georgia, to Banner Elk in 1872 to become the area's first dentist.

The Hudson brothers, Monroe and Johnny, moved to Caldwell County in the 1800s from South Carolina. Monroe Hudson was the first postmaster and probably was responsible for the Hudsonville name first given to the town of Hudson. Folks discontinued the "ville" after a few years. Postmaster Hudson lived in the building where he ran a grocery store along with the post office.

Folks said Johnny Hudson attended church every time the doors opened and was just about the most religious person they knew. He was uncomplicated, laid back, and likable, and maybe that's why Johnny lived to be a very old man. When his first wife died, he married her sister. The town name was as much for one brother as the other, the story goes.

Others say the town, which was incorporated in 1905, wasn't named for Monroe and Johnny Hudson at all, but for a David Hudson, who founded the town.

Folks have forgotten the first names of the two Duncan brothers from Seaforth, Ontario, in Canada, who came to Harnett County as construction workers with the Durham & Southern Railroad around 1900. They aren't sure either how the town of Casma on NC 42 near the Wake County line came to be named for them. Doesn't really matter because the name was changed back to Casma by 1930 because the townspeoples' mail kept ending up in Duncan, South Carolina. Where the name Casma came from is not known either.

In 1872, the Wade brothers owned the store that housed the new post office in a Montgomery County town, so it came to be called Wadeville.

Have North Carolinians ignored the two-party political system when it came to place names? Could we have been amiss with our political correctness? Perish the thought.

Look no further than Democrat Community in Buncombe County, and Democrat Community on the Madison-Yancey County line. You'll find Republican Community in Bertie County, although to be factual, the name came from Republican Baptist Church, and the church got its name from the public meeting place nature of the church.

But who's being picky?

Part V

County Names

Origins of County Names

Alamance: For the Battle of Alamance, May 16, 1771, or Alamance Creek—the word probably came with early German settlers—"Alemanni" (a Rhineland region), or a Saxhapaw Indian word "alamons," meaning "noisy river."

Alexander: For Legislator William Julius Alexander.

Alleghany: Delaware Indian word, meaning either "a fine stream" or "endless," or named for the Allegewi Indian tribe.

Anson: For George Anson (1697-1762), first Lord of the British Admiralty.

Ashe: For Samuel Ashe (1725-1813), Revolutionary patriot, governor 1795-98.

Avery: For Colonel Waightstill Avery, Revolutionary soldier and first attorney general. Once challenged to a duel by Andrew Jackson, Avery allowed Jackson to fire at him and miss. Then instead of shooting Jackson, Avery lectured him on the foolhardiness of dueling.

Beaufort: For Henry Somerset, English Duke of Beaufort, a Lord Proprietor.

Bertie: Named for James (1673-1735) and Henry Bertie, (1675-

1735) Lords Proprietors, younger sons of a noble English family.

Bladen: For Martin Bladen (1680-1746), English Controller of the Mint and Commissioner of Trade and Plantations.

Brunswick: For King George I, Duke of Brunswick.

Buncombe: For Colonel Edward Buncombe, who came from St. Kitts in the West Indies to Tyrrell county in 1776, where he built a fifty-five-room mansion he named Buncombe Hall. Revolutionary War soldier.

Burke: For Thomas Burke, who emigrated to America because of a family quarrel in Ireland. Governor from 1781 to 1782.

Cabarrus: For Stephen Cabarrus, (1754-1808) Legislative Speaker in 1792, voted for formation of new county from Mecklenburg.

Caldwell: For Dr. Joseph Caldwell (1773-1835), president of University of North Carolina.

Camden: For Sir Charles Pratt, Earl of Camden (1716-1794), English political leader who opposed the Stamp Act.

Carteret: For Sir John Carteret, Earl of Granville (1690-1763), a Lord Proprietor.

Caswell: For Revolutionary soldier Richard Caswell (1729-1789), first governor.

Catawba: Formed in 1842 from Lincoln County and named for Catawba Indians who lived here.

Chatham: For William Pitt, Earl of Chatham. Pitt County was also named for him.

Cherokee: For Cherokee Indians. County formed 1839 from lands obtained by the treaty of New Echota.

Chowan: For the Chowan River, Indian name from Chowanoke tribe meaning "people of the south."

Clay: For Henry Clay (1777-1852), patriot and orator.

Cleveland: For Revolutionary soldier, Colonel Benjamin Cleaveland (spelling changed in 1885 when Grover Cleveland became president).

Columbus: For Christopher Columbus.

Craven: In honor of one of the three Williams, Earls of Craven, who were successively Lords Proprietors.

Cumberland: For Prince William Augustus, Duke of Cumberland (1721-1765), second son of English King George II, who commanded English troops at the Battle of Culloden in 1746.

Currituck: From Indian word, "coratank," meaning "geese."

Dare: For Virginia Dare (1587-?) first child of English parents born in America.

Davidson: For Revolutionary General William Lee Davidson, killed in the Battle of Chowan's Ford on the Catawba in 1781.

Davie: For William Richardson Davie (1756-1820), Revolutionary soldier, governor, minister to France, and a founder of the University of North Carolina.

Duplin: For Thomas Hay, Lord Duplin (1710-1787), member of the English Board of Trade and Plantations.

Durham: For the town of Durham, named for Dr. Bartlett Leonidas Durham, who donated land for the railroad station there.

Edgecombe: For Richard Edgecumbe (1680-1750), Baron Edgecumbe, English Lord of the Treasury and member of Parliament.

Forsyth: For a brave militia soldier of the War of 1812, Colonel Benjamin Forsyth.

Franklin: For Benjamin Franklin (1706-1790), who was a successful printer, author, scientist, diplomat, and statesman.

Gaston: For William Gaston (1778-1844), U.S. congressman and North Carolina Supreme Court judge.

Gates: For Revolutionary General Horatio Gates, whose victory over Burgoyne at Saratoga inspired the naming of this county in 1779.

Graham: For William A. Graham (1804-1875), U.S. senator, governor, secretary of the Navy, and Confederate States senator.

Granville: For John Carteret (1690-1763), Earl of Granville.

Greene: For General Nathanael Greene (1742-1786), Revolutionary soldier.

Guilford: For Francis North, first Earl of Guilford (1704-1790), English attorney general and member of Parliament.

Halifax: For George Montagu, second Earl of Halifax (1716-1771), president of the English Board of Trade and Plantations, English secretary of state, and Lord Lieutenant of Ireland.

Harnett: For Colonial legislator Cornelius Harnett (1723-1781), Revolutionary patriot, author of the Halifax Resolves, and delegate to the Continental Congress.

Haywood: For State Treasurer John Haywood (1787-1827).

Henderson: For Chief Justice of the N.C. Supreme Court, Leonard Henderson (1773-1833)--had no known connection to the area and had been dead five years when the county was created in 1838.

Hertford: For Francis Seymour Conway, Marquis of Hertford (1719-1794), English Lord of the Bed Chamber and Knight of the Garter,

Privy Chancellor of Iredell and ambassador to France.

Hoke: For Confederate Major General Robert F. Hoke (1837-1912).

Hyde: First named Wickham Precinct when formed in 1705, name changed to Hyde about 1712, honoring Governor Edward Hyde who died in 1712.

Iredell: For Jurist James Iredell (1751-1799), attorney general of N.C. and delegate to the Constitutional Convention of 1788. His son, James Iredell, Jr., became governor in 1827.

Jackson: For Andrew Jackson, seventh president of the United States.

Johnston: For Governor Gabriel Johnston (1699-1752).

Jones: For Willie Jones, patriot and anti-Federalist leader during first days of the republic. His influence figured in the Convention of 1788's failure to ratify the Federal Constitution.

Lee: For General Robert E. Lee (1807-70).

Lenoir: For Revolutionary General William Lenoir (1751-1839).

Lincoln: For Revolutionary General Benjamin Lincoln (1733-1810).

McDowell: For Revolutionary soldier and physician, Joseph McDowell, first U. S. congressman from Western North Carolina.

Macon: For Nathaniel Macon, Jeffersonian Republican who sat in Congress for thirty-seven years. He said that five dollars a day was ample pay for a congressman and believed that government's sole purpose should be policing protection of life and property.

Madison: For James Madison (1751-1836), fourth President of the United States.

Martin: For Josiah Martin (1737-1786), last royal governor of North Carolina.

Mecklenburg: For Princess Charlotte Sophia of Mecklenburg-Strelitz (German queen of George III), name given in 1762.

Mitchell: For Dr. Elisha Mitchell, scientist and professor at the University of North Carolina, who in 1835 measured the peak now known as Mount Mitchell and discovered it to be the highest in Eastern America.

Montgomery: For Revolutionary General Richard Montgomery (1736-75).

Moore: For Revolutionary Captain Alfred Moore, who later became an U.S. Supreme Court justice.

Nash: For Revolutionary General Francis Nash (1742-77).

New Hanover: In honor of English King, George I, who also ruled the Kingdom of Hanover, Germany.

Northhampton: For James Compton (1687-1754), Earl of Northampton.

Onslow: For Arthur Onslow, British legislator, speaker of House of Commons for 33 years—longest tenure in history of Parliament.

Orange: Probably named for infant William V (1748-1806) of Orange, grandson of English King George III, Stadholder of the Netherlands.

Pamlico: County named for Pamlico Sound, which was named for Pamlico Indians of the area.

Pasquotank: Indian word "pask-e'tan-ki," meaning "where the current divides or forks."

Pender: For William Dorsey Pender (1834-63), youngest major general of the Confederacy.

Perquimans: Named for Indians who lived in the area.

Person: For Revolutionary War Brigadier General Thomas Person, legislator, charter trustee of University of North Carolina.

Pitt: For William Pitt, Earl of Chatham—Chatham County also named for him.

Polk: For Revolutionary Colonel William Polk (1758-1834), who was the last surviving field officer of the North Carolina line.

Randolph: For Peyton Randolph, first president of Continental Congress (1774-75).

Richmond: For Charles Lennox (1735-1806), third Duke of Richmond, English secretary of state who denounced British Colonial policy.

Robeson: For Revolutionary Colonel and State Senator Thomas Robeson. In 1787 when county formed, Robeson opposed creating the new county creation from his own, Bladen, until suggestion that the new county have his name.

Rockingham: For Charles Watson-Wentworth (1730-1782), second Marquis of Rockingham, supporter of American independence.

Rowan: For Matthew Rowan, acting governor at time county formed in 1753.

Rutherford: For Revolutionary General Griffin Rutherford.

Sampson: For Revolutionary Colonel and Legislator John Sampson (?-1784), member of House of Commons.

Scotland: For Kingdom of Scotland in the British Isles, former home of many early settlers.

Stanly: For John Stanly (1774-1834), member of General Assembly, speaker of House of Commons and member of Congress.

Stokes: For Revolutionary Colonel John Stokes, elder brother of

Governor Montford Stokes. Appointed District Judge of the U.S. by President George Washington and held the first United States Federal Court in North Carolina.

Surry: For Lord Surrey, member of Parliament who protested the heavy taxation of the colonies—or for the English county of Surrey, birthplace of incumbent royal governor, William Tryon—or possibly influenced by Saura Indians who lived in the region.

Swain: For David Lowrie Swain, educator and governor at age thirty-one. Swain was first lawyer of Buncombe County and had two nicknames—"Old Warping Ars" and "Old Bunk."

Transylvania: Name comes from two Latin words, "trans" (across) and "sylva" (woods).

Tyrrell: For Sir John Tyrrell (1685-1729), who became a Lord Proprietor by purchasing Sir Anthony Ashley Cooper's share in the colony, then sold it to Archibald Hutcheson, who in turn returned it to George II in 1728.

Union: For the union of parts of two counties, Anson and Mecklenburg, or for the union of the states.

Vance: For Zebulon Baird Vance (1830-1894), governor, U.S. congressman, and U.S. senator.

Wake: Named in 1771 for Margaret Wake Tryon, Governor Tryon's wife.

Warren: For Joseph Warren, Massachusetts doctor who spearheaded the Boston patriots and died in the Battle of Bunker Hill.

Washington: For President George Washington (1732-1799).

Watauga: For Watauga River. Name is Creek Indian word meaning "broken waters," or a Cherokee word with various interpretations: "beautiful waters, river of islands, land beyond." Or could be named for an Indian tribe.

Wayne: For Revolutionary General Anthony Wayne, whose courage and daring activities earned him the nickname of "Mad Anthony."

Wilkes: For John Wilkes (1727-1797), English member of Parliament who supported American rights during the Revolution.

Wilson: For Louis Dicken Wilson, State Senator from Edgecombe for fifteen terms and Mexican War martyr.

Yadkin: Pee Dee Indian word meaning quiet, peaceful, or perhaps just the opposite with "yeatkin," a challenging word meaning "come over and fight."

Yancey: For Legislator Bartlett Yancey (1785-1828), one of the first to favor public schools.

Part VI

Sources and Credits

Heritage Books

Allen, W. M. "Elkin." *Heritage Book of Surry County*, Vol.I. Dobson, N. C.: Genealogical Association of Surry County, 1983.

Austin, Shirley. "Corolla." *The Journal of Currituck County Historical Society*, Vol.I. no.3. Barco, N. C.: Currituck County Historical Society, Inc., 1976.

Billings, Bill. "Shakerag." (from the Centennial Edition of the 1982 *Courier Times*,) *Heritage Book of Person County*, Vol.1. Roxboro, N. C.: Historical Society of Person County, 1981.

Bizzell, Oscar. "Slapout," "Falcon," "Spivey's Corner," "Easy Street." *Heritage Book of Sampson County.* Newton Grove, N. C.: The Historical Society of Sampson County, 1983.

Blount, Ruth Siler. "Texana." *Heritage Book of Cherokee County,* Vol. I. Murphy, N. C.: Historical Association of Cherokee County, 1987.

Brown, Joan. "Wayah Bald." *Heritage Book of Macon County.* Franklin, N. C.: Historical Society of Macon County, 1987.

Cabaniss, Jeff, Dawn Delk, Denise Martin, students, Peggy Wells, teacher. "Ellenboro." *Heritage Book of Rutherford County*, Vol. I. Forest City, N. C.: Old Tryon County Genealogical Society, 1984.
Casstevens, Frances H. "Boonville," "Lone Hickory." *Heritage Book*

of Yadkin County. Yadkinville, N. C.: Historical and Genealogical Society of Yadkin County, 1981.

"Claremont," "Longview." (from *Observer-News Enterprize*) *Heritage Book of Catawba County.* Hickory, N. C.: Genealogical Society of Catawba County, 1986.

Doxey, Jean D., Margaret Walker, Barbara B. Snowden. "Maple." *The Journal of Currituck County Historical Society*, Vol. I, no.3. Barco, N. C.: Currituck County Historical Society, 1976.

Elks, Alice Mills. "Black Jack." *Heritage Book of Pitt County.* Greenville, N. C.: Pitt County Historical Society, Inc., 1982.

Flowers, John Baxton, III. "Mount Olive," "Eureka." *Heritage Book of Wayne County.* Goldsboro, N. C.: Wayne County Historical Association and Old Dobbs County Genealogical Society, 1982.

"Four Oaks." *Heritage Book of Johnston County.* Smithfield, N. C.: Historical Association of Johnston County, 1983.

Gosnell, James Richard. "Joe," "Trust." *Heritage Book of Old Buncombe County*, Vol. I. Asheville, N. C.: Old Buncombe Genealogical Society, Inc., 1981.

Hartley, Margaret, Watson Wilson, Alma McGimsey, Mary Alice Ballew. "Nebo." *Heritage Book of McDowell County.* Nebo, N. C.: McDowell Genealogical Society, 1993.

Hodges, Correy. "Wondertown." *Heritage Book of Harnett County*, Vol. I. Erwin, N. C.: Historical Society of Harnett County, 1993.

Houck, Mrs. Connie D. (with part of her information coming from Mrs. Ed M. Anderson's August 6th, 1959 article in *The Skyland Post*) "Crumpler and Healing Springs." *Heritage Book of Ashe County*, Vol. I. West Jefferson, N.C.: Historical Society Inc.of Ashe County, 1984.

Jenkins, Hazel. "Yonah." *Heritage Book of Swain County.* Bryson

City, N. C.: The Genealogical and Historical Society of Swain County, 1988.

Johnson, Emily C. "Buffalo Ford." *Heritage Book of Randolph County*, Vol. I. Asheboro, N. C.: Genealogical Society of Randolph County, 1993.

Kluttz, Mabel Peeler. "Rockwell." *Heritage Book of Rowan County*, Vol. I. Salisbury, N. C.: Genealogical Society of Rowan County, 1991.

Landreth, Lou Reid. "Gap Civil." *Heritage Book of Alleghany County*. Sparta, N. C.: Historical-Genealogical Society, Inc., 1983.

Lane, Mildred. "Bertha." *The Journal of Currituck County Historical Society*, Vol. I, no. 3. Barco, N. C.: Currituck County Historical Society, 1976.

Lovingood, Willie, Quentin, and Mamie, Annie Mae DeWeese, John Parris in *Asheville Citizen*, White and Davis Family Records. "Hanging Dog." *Heritage Book of Cherokee County*, Vol. I. Murphy, N. C.: Historical Association of Cherokee County, 1987.

Lukei, Melinda Jones. "Wash Woods." *Heritage Book of Currituck County*. Currituck, N. C.: Albemarle Genealogical Society, Inc. and Currituck Historical Society, Inc., 1985.

McCullen, Joseph T. "Sharecake." (from his grandfather, Jerry Gore) *Heritage Book of Sampson County*. Newton Grove, N.C.: The Historical Society of Sampson County, 1983.

Mode, Wilma, Jeanette Jarette. "Community Names." (from Glenwood Elementary School Self-Study-1977) *Heritage Book Of McDowell County*, Nebo, N.C.: McDowell Genealogical Society, 1993.

"Mooresville." (from *Mooresville Tribune*, Lyn Sullivan, Editor) *Heritage Book of Iredell County*. Statesville, N. C.: Genealogical Society of Iredell, 1980.

Murray, George M. "Burrtown." *Heritage Book of Cleveland County.* Shelby, N. C.: Cleveland County Historical Society, 1982.

Neal, Joseph W. "Meadows." *Heritage Book of Stokes County,* Vol. I. Germanton, N. C.: Historical Society of Stokes County, 1981.

Nicholson, Fannie, and Hazel Banks Adams. "Comfort." *History and Genealogy of Jones County.* Trenton, N. C.: Julia Pollock Harriett, Editor and Publisher, 1987.

Parker, Helen L. "Harmony." *Heritage Book of Iredell County.* Statesville, N. C.: Genealogical Society of Iredell, 1980.

Perry, Mrs. Joseph A., "Justice," Lib Cheatham, "Youngsville," *SPECIAL 100 ANNIVERSARY ISSUE, THE FRANKLIN TIMES,* July 30, 1970. Louisburg, N. C.: Publisher, Gary Cunard.

Poteat, Carolyn Kluttz. "Bear Poplar," "Mt. Ulla." *Heritage Book of Rowan County,* Vol. I. Salisbury, N. C.: Genealogical Society of Rowan County, 1991.

Rollins, T. A. "Christian Light," "Cokesbury." *Heritage Book of Harnett County,* Vol. I. Erwin, N. C.: Historical Society of Harnett County, 1993.

Roy, Janice. "Abner," "Black Ankle." (in articles for the *Montgomery Herald*) *Heritage Book of Montgomery County,* Vol. II. Troy, N. C.: Montgomery County Historical Society, 1992.

Sawyer, Roy E. "Kilmarlic." *Heritage Book of Currituck County.* Currituck, N. C.: Albemarle Genealogical Society, Inc. and Currituck Historical Society, Inc., 1985.

Sifford, Harry T. "Faith." *Heritage Book of Rowan County,* Vol. I. Salisbury, N. C.: Genealogical Society of Rowan County, 1991.

Stephens, Kay Roberts. "Salter Path." (from Alice Smith's Memoirs) *Heritage Book of Carteret County,* Vol. I. Morehead City, N. C.: Carteret County Historical Society,Inc., 1982.

Stickel, Pearl Barnette. "Vashti." *Heritage Book of Alexander County*, Vol. I. Hiddenite, N. C.: Alexander County Ancestry Association, Inc., 1986.

Surratt, Carlos. "Toast." *Heritage Book of Surry County*, Vol. I. Dobson, N. C.: Genealogical Association of Surry County, 1983.

Tate, Mildred. "Pleasant Gardens." *Heritage Book of McDowell County*. Nebo, N. C.: McDowell Genealogical Society, 1993.

Taylor, Michael G. "Oak City." *Heritage Book of Martin County*. Williamston, N. C.: Martin County Historical Society, Inc., 1980.

Twombly, Birdie W. "Barium Springs." *Heritage Book of Iredell County*. Statesville, N. C.: Genealogical Society of Iredell, 1980.

Watson, June C. "Gold Hill," "Barber." *Heritage Book of Rowan County*, Vol. I. Salisbury, N. C.: Genealogical Society of Rowan County, 1991.

Wikle, John. "Japan." *Heritage Book of Swain County*. Bryson City, N. C.: The Genealogical and Historical Society of Swain County, 1988.

Wilson, Hazel, Lois Jennings, and Alvin Adams. "Union Grove." *Heritage Book of Iredell County*. Statesville, N. C.: Genealogical Society of Iredell, 1980.

Wynne, Harry. "Beargrass." *Heritage Book of Martin County*. Williamston,N.C.:Martin County Historcal Society, Inc., 1980.

Other Works

American Guide Series, The Federal Writers' Project of the Federal Works Agency. *North Carolina The WPA Guide to the Old North State*. First Publishing, Chapel Hill, N. C.: Univ. of North Carolina Press, 1939, Second Publishing, Columbia, S. C.: Univ. of South Carolina Press, 1988.

Arthur, John Parker. *History of Western North Carolina 1730-1913* (reproduced from a 1914 edition in the NC Collection, UNC, Chapel Hill, published by the Edward Buncombe Chapter of the D.A.R., Asheville) Reprinted 1973, The Reprint Co., Spartanburg, S. C.

Cooper, Horton. *History of Avery County North Carolina*. Asheville, N. C.: Biltmore Press, 1964.

Huneycutt, James E. and Ida C. *The History of Richmond County*. Raleigh, N. C.: Edwards and Broughton Publishers, 1976.

Powell, William S. *The North Carolina Gazetteer*. Chapel Hill, N. C.: The University of North Carolina Press, 1968.

Ray, Lenoir. *POSTMARKS, A HISTORY OF HENDERSON COUNTY, NORTH CAROLINA 1787-1968*. Chicago: Adams Press, 1970.

Sharpe, Bill. 1954-1965. *A New Geography of North Carolina*. 4 vols. Raleigh, N. C.: Sharpe Publishing Company.

Wellman, Manly Wade. *The County of Moore, 1847-1947*. Carthage, N. C.: Moore County Historical Association, 1962.

Additional Resources

Perry, Mrs. Joseph A., "Justice," Lib Cheatham, "Youngsville," *SPECIAL 100 ANNIVERSARY ISSUE, THE FRANKLIN TIMES.* July 30, 1970. Louisburg, N. C.: Publisher, Gary Cunard.

Aulis, Jack. "Silk Hope." *The State Magazine, Down Home in North Carolina.* March, 1986, Raleigh, N. C.: W. B. Wright, Publisher.

Friday, Sarah. "Fuquay-Varina." *The State Magazine, Down Home in North Carolina.* July, 1994, and "Lizard Lick," December, 1993, Charlotte, N. C.: Sam Rogers, Publisher.

Goerch, Carl. "Ahoskie." *The State Magazine.* vol. 36, no. 3, page 4, July 1, 1968, Bill Sharpe, Publisher, Raleigh, N. C.

King, Walter E. "Ellerbe." *The State Magazine, Down Home in North Carolina.* February, 1994, Charlotte, N. C.: Sam Rogers, Publisher.

McKinnon, Henry A. Jr. "Maxton." *The State Magazine, Down Home in North Carolina.* November, 1984, Raleigh, N. C.: W. B. Wright, Publisher.

Pitts, Marjorie. "Brookford." *Hickory Daily Record*, reprinted in the *Statesville Record and Landmark* on November 7,1994, Statesville, N. C.